GUIDE TO CIVIL WAR
PHILADELPHIA

GUIDE TO CIVIL WAR
PHILADELPHIA

RICHARD A. SAUERS

DA CAPO PRESS
A Member of the Perseus Books Group

Designed by C. Cairl Design
Cataloging-in-Publication data for this book is available from the Library of Congress.
First Da Capo Press edition 2003
ISBN 0–306–81232–0

Published by Da Capo Press
A Member of the Perseus Books Group
http://www.dacapopress.com
Da Capo Press books are available at special discounts for bulk purchases in the U.S. by corporations, institutions, and other organizations. For more information, please contact the Special Markets Department at the Perseus Books Group, 11 Cambridge Center, Cambridge, MA 02142, or call (800) 255-1514, or (617) 252–5298, or e-mail j.mccrary@perseusbooks.com.

1 2 3 4 5 6 7 8 9—05 04 03

Contents

Acknowledgments

This guide would not have been possible without the generous assistance of a host of individuals. In addition to those listed here, many more kind folks whose names I did not obtain also helped to answer questions as I finished this project.

Michael Angelo, Independence Seaport Museum; Bruce S. Bazelon, Pennsylvania Historical and Museum Commission, Harrisburg; Richard Boardman, Free Library of Philadelphia; Trudy Carroll, Delaware County Historical Society; Michael Cavanaugh, Philadelphia; Rhonda Cooper, Woodlands Cemetery; Doris Dysinger, Bucknell University, Lewisburg, PA; Linda I. Flook-Birnbaum, Beverly National Cemetery; Ted Goldsborough, Lower Merion Historical Society; Mary Alice Hamilton, Bed & Breakfast Connections; Mark Hankin, Arsenal Business Center; Anita Hart, Riverside Cemetery; Ruthann Hubbert Kemper, PA Capitol Preservation Committee; Roger Hunt, Rockville, MD; Liz Jarvis, Chestnut Hill Historical Society; Nina Long, Wistar Institute; Nancy Lynch, Independence Seaport Museum; Howard Michael Madaus, Harrisburg; Blake Magner, Westmont, NJ; Jay Nachman, National Museum of American Jewish History; J. Craig Nannos, Villanova, PA; Crystal Anderson Polis, American

Swedish Historical Museum; Laura Robb, Historical Society of the Phoenixville Area; Leonard and Edie Siegel, Bala Cynwyd, PA; Alice Smith, Historical Society of Montgomery County; Teresa Stuhlman, Fairmount Park; Perry Triplett, La Mott, PA; David Ward, Lakeville, CT; Dr. Andy Waskie, Philadelphia; Margaret Williams, Rector, Memorial Church of St. Luke the Beloved Physician; Steven Wright, Philadelphia; Susan Wright, Christ Church; Ka-Kee Yan, Pennsylvania Academy of Fine Arts.

All photographs in this book, with the exception of the Horstmann Factory woodcut, were taken by local photographer Meredith Hill. The print of the Horstmann Factory was provided by the Pennsylvania Capitol Preservation Committee, with the original in the Pennsylvania State Archives.

Introduction

When the Civil War began in 1861, the City of Philadelphia was one of the most important centers of industry behind the Northern war effort. Two federal arsenals furnished ammunition and other materiel, while the Naval Yard built and repaired vessels. Other factories included one of the country's largest locomotive builders and one of the busiest flag manufacturers. One of the city's bankers successfully marketed government bonds and raised millions for the Lincoln administration. Several prominent Union generals were born in Philadelphia, while the flower of the city's manhood, clothed in blue uniforms, went off to fight the Confederacy. The area cemeteries provide stark visualization of the sacrifices made during those four bloody years. Philadelphia, long a center of abolitionist ferment, provided safe havens for escaping slaves via the Underground Railroad. Later, from 1863 to 1865, a recruitment camp for black soldiers was established near the city.

While the ravages of time and modernization have erased much of wartime Philadelphia, a number of Civil War landmarks still survive. A quarter of a century ago, it was estimated that perhaps 2,000 eighteenth-century homes still stood in the city and its suburbs; scores of nineteenth-century buildings from the Civil War era also remain to be seen. This guidebook, the first of its kind, provides the interested Civil War tourist and researcher a varied palette of information. Museums, archives and libraries provide scholars and buffs alike with treasure troves of research material. A number of museums contain excellent Civil War collections within their walls. Cemeteries include numerous Union officers, Confederate prisoners and thousands of Union soldiers. Commemorative statues and plaques abound throughout the city. Even Independence Hall, one of the country's most important Revolutionary War landmarks, has a connection to the events of the 1860s.

This book includes an overview of the city's wartime history, directions for reaching the sites mentioned in this guide and a selected list of accommodations that have Civil War connections. The bibliography allows readers to delve further into the Civil War history of Philadelphia and its troops.

CIVIL WAR PHILADELPHIA:
A BRIEF HISTORY

Named for a Greek city in Asia Minor, Philadelphia ("City of Brotherly Love") was founded in 1681 when agents of the English Quaker William Penn bought land between the Delaware and Schuylkill Rivers from the Lenni-Lenape Indians. Penn envisioned a city of wide-open green spaces with a regular grid of streets where people of every faith would live and work together in harmony. As a result, Philadelphia and Penn's colony of Pennsylvania attracted a wide range of ethnic groups and religious faiths.

Philadelphia was the colonies' second-largest city when the Revolution began in 1775. Although occupied by British forces for part of the war, the city survived largely intact. The Continental Congress met in the city, where also the 1787 Constitutional Convention met to replace the Articles of Confederation with a new U.S. Constitution. Philadelphia acted as the young nation's capital from 1790 to 1800 and as state capital until 1799.

Throughout the first half of the nineteenth century, Philadelphia continued to expand. Penn had originally drafted a city where the streets ran at right angles to one another and that contained four major squares as well as a central square. By the time of the Civil War, the city had grown past these squares as industrialization transformed Penn's dream of an orderly green city into something completely different. Thousands of immigrants deluged the new factories springing up, which led to the growth of slums and at times clashes and ethnic tensions, culminating in the widespread 1844 riots between Irish immigrants and the Know-Nothing Party.

In spite of such tensions, the city's economic and social base continued to grow. Girard College was established in 1848, and in 1850, the city police force was begun. In 1851, the Shakespeare Society and the Spring Garden Institute opened their doors.

Due to the tumultuous rioting of the 1840s, politicians began to notice that the city proper, which in 1850 only counted some 121,000 people, needed to be consolidated with adjacent political units. In early 1854, the state legislature passed the Act of Consolidation, by which the city's boundaries were extended to include all of Philadelphia County. As a result, the city's population suddenly jumped to more than 360,000, but a proper city government could now be organized. An important step toward regulating the city was the introduction of regular house numbers in 1856, a trend copied in other large cities. Many streets were renamed to provide continuity within the boundaries of the new, larger city.

Except for national "panics" (depressions), the consolidation of the city meant prosperous years ahead. Fairmount Park was expanded, and in 1856, the fledgling Republican Party held its first national convention in the city. The Academy of Music opened in 1857, and the Zoological Society was founded in 1859. Even though the Panic of 1857 affected city businesses, railroad construction continued unabated, with more than fourteen charters granted in 1858 alone.

By 1860, Philadelphia's population had swelled to 565,529, making it the second largest city in America (after New York) and perhaps the fourth largest city in Western civilization; only London and Paris were larger.

Some problems, however, were developing within Philadelphia. Railroads threading their way through the city proved dangerous to both pedestrians and vehicles owing to numerous unregulated crossings. Eighteen street railway companies (early trolleys) competed to carry the daily load of 46,000 riders through the city's main streets that often were neglected morasses of mud.

The influx of immigrants meant crowded slums that coalesced around the edge of the growing city–Moyamensing, Passyunk, Spring Garden, Penn and Kensington in particular. Since the city was not that old in terms of growth, the new residents were unable to find an adequate stock of older homes; in many cases, the urban poor resorted to squatting or building their own substandard shacks. The middle and upper classes lived in the area of Chestnut, Walnut, Spruce and Pine Streets.

The city's 1860s equivalent of the main business district centered from Third to Eighth Streets and from Walnut to Market. Unlike in modern central business districts, in 1860 many stores were interspersed among small manufacturing businesses. The larger factories were generally located near or just beyond the city limits. These industries—some textile, gas fixture, locomotive, umbrella, brick and ironworks—were located near the slums in which many of the working-class poor lived. Small-business own-

ers such as milliners, tailors, shoemakers, bookbinders and print-
ers were still located "downtown." Textile mills lined the Delaware
River just north of the city.

Philadelphia was considered by many in the North to be
closely tied to the South, and indeed the city's economic ties to
the South were numerous. Area factories and businesses brought
in lumber, turpentine and cotton from Southern states while
shipping out sundry items such as locomotives, bibles, school-
books, wagons, carriages, shoes and clothes. Even as late as the
firing on Fort Sumter in April 1861, trainloads of consumer
goods were en route to Southern customers. More than half of
the students enrolled in the city's medical schools came from
south of the Mason-Dixon line. Although the city was headquarters for a number of antislavery societies and possessed a
strong Quaker influence, the slave question was not a topic that
agitated most Philadelphians. Abolitionists were held in low
esteem, and the city was the scene of several public disturbances
against the abolition movement.

But the firing on Fort Sumter galvanized the city's populace.
Within hours of reading the early newspaper accounts of the
attack, patriotic mobs roamed through the streets, intimidating
those who dared to declare their Southern sympathies and forcing recalcitrant newspaper editors to display the national flag as
a show of support.

When President Lincoln announced the call for 75,000
three-month militia to suppress the rebellion, Philadelphia
responded with an overwhelming show of support. Within a hec-
tic ten-day period, the state raised and equipped twenty-five regiments of infantry. Philadelphia's contribution totaled eight regiments, the 17th through the 24th. Throughout the conflict, the
city sent thousands of men in blue off to war. Some of the more
famous units included the Philadelphia Brigade (the 69th, 71st,

72nd and 106th Regiments), 2nd Reserves (31st Infantry), 6th Cavalry (Rush's Lancers), 95th Infantry (Gosline's Zouaves), 114th Infantry (Collis's Zouaves) and 118th Infantry (organized by the Corn Exchange). The city's German population supplied the bulk of the 73rd, 75th and 98th Regiments. In addition to the entire 69th Infantry, Irishmen comprised the 116th Infantry and quite a number of the 13th Cavalry.

Philadelphia was a leading textile center in 1861, with more than 300 separate firms ranging from small to large. Many of these firms were able to adapt to the loss of cotton and switched to wool, thus garnering many government contracts. The Schuylkill Arsenal supplied all clothing for the regular army when the war began. To keep up with suddenly increased demand, the army quartermaster authorized the beginning of an elaborate system of subcontracting. When the army published bids for contracts, ofttimes the successful bidders subcontracted out much of the work, and thus a web of smaller suppliers worked together to furnish materials for the larger bidders. At times, these middlemen were involved in fraudulent transactions, but on the whole the system seemed to work well.

Soon after the war began, Pennsylvania Quartermaster General Reuben C. Hale arrived in Philadelphia and discovered that the Schuylkill Arsenal could not meet his demands for uniforms for state troops. He therefore established an emergency clothing depot in the Girard House, a vacant hotel across the street from the newer Continental Hotel. Hundreds of local women, ranging from the city's elite to the working class, swarmed to work sewing uniforms; in less than ten weeks they produced more than 10,000 uniforms.

Philadelphia was also becoming a rail center by the early 1860s. A number of railroads entered the city; each had a depot where passengers congregated while waiting for trains. Railroading was yet to mature across America, so many of the lines did not interconnect. As a result, passengers transferring from one line to another had to journey between depots. In April 1861, the depots in the city consisted of the following.

- ☞ New York lines–Walnut Street Wharf
- ☞ Baltimore and Washington lines–Broad and Prime Streets
- ☞ Pennsylvania Central–Thirtieth and Market Streets
- ☞ Philadelphia and Reading–Broad and Callowhill Streets
- ☞ West Chester and Media–Thirty-first and Market Streets
- ☞ Philadelphia, Germantown and Norristown–Ninth and Green Streets
- ☞ North Pennsylvania–Third and Thompson Streets

From the start, Philadelphia businesses rallied behind the war effort. Many retooled in an effort to obtain lucrative government contracts. Companies that had never manufactured military goods suddenly tried to learn how, either by doing it themselves or obtaining contracts then subcontracting to fill the orders. Alfred W. Adolph, a hatter located on North Second Street, had been in business since 1848. When war came, his firm, then called Adolph & Keen, landed many excellent government contracts for army hats totaling more than 200,000 pieces. William P. Wilstach & Company manufactured saddlery hardware prior to the war. His firm branched out and secured contracts for brass eagles and hat letters and numbers, belt plates, currycombs, spurs and picket pins. Dozens of other firms cashed in on the war and throughout the conflict Philadelphia was a manufacturing hub.

Two United States arsenals were located in the city. The Frankford Arsenal, located just north of the mouth of Frankford Creek where it flowed into the Delaware River, had grown to fifty-nine acres by 1861. A central parade ground was surrounded by a barracks, two storehouses, two larger buildings, a hospital, powder magazine and smaller workshops. This arsenal manufactured ammunition and performed experiments on newer equipment. The Schuylkill Arsenal, located on the Gray's Ferry Road, was by 1861 a repository and collection point for clothing and general military equipage.

Since there were relatively few large weapons manufacturers in America in 1861, the government subcontracted much of its weapons needs. A few Philadelphia firearms makers obtained lucrative contracts throughout the war. Chief among them was the firm of Alfred Jenks & Son, located in Bridesburg near the Frankford Arsenal. Jenks had started the Bridesburg Machine Works in the 1820s. In 1861, his son Barton and a partner converted the plant to make weapons, producing 98,464 Springfield rifle muskets.

Christian Sharps moved to Philadelphia in 1857 and organized C. Sharps & Company, which produced Sharps breechloading and self-priming pistols as well as Sharps rifles. In 1863, Sharps and William C. Hankins formed Sharps & Hankins and continued producing weapons. The firm was located on Thirtieth Street south of Bridge in West Philadelphia.

Other weapons producers included James Henry & Son. James inherited his father's armaments business in 1836 and brought in his son Granville in 1860. The firm produced Henry rifles. John H. Krider, a gunsmith working since 1820, also received government contracts for rifles. The firm of George J. Richardson & William W. Overman contracted for more than 17,000 Gallagher percussion carbines. Other firms supplied parts for arms makers across the North. Such firms included C. H. Williams & Company (who supplied locks) and Morris, Tasker & Company (barrels).

Just outside Philadelphia was the small town of Phoenixville. Here was located the Phoenix Iron Works that during the war produced 3-inch ordnance rifles, a primary rifled cannon of the federal armies. Several firms, among them Dickson & Zane, North, Chase & North, and Savery & Company, churned out tens of thousands of artillery projectiles.

Several Philadelphia businesses supplied cavalry sabers, artillery swords, noncommissioned officers' swords and musicians' swords. Chief among these was the prestigious firm of Horstmann Brothers & Company, which also garnered many contracts to produce flags for the army as well as for several states. Philip S. Justice, William P. Wilstach, Joseph C. Grubb and H. G. Leisenring also contributed thousands of swords to the cause.

The United States Navy had a navy yard in Philadelphia. Opened in 1800, the eighteen-acre yard featured two large ship houses and eventually employed up to 3,000 workers. A number of private shipyards also received building contracts for naval vessels. Chief among these were William Cramp & Sons, Neafie & Levy, Hillman & Streaker, John W. Lynn, and Jacob Birely. Reany, Son & Archbold, located in Chester, south of the city on the Delaware River, also built ships for the navy. The firm of Merrick & Sons provided engines for these new warships.

In January 1861, Jay Cooke and William G. Moorhead organized the firm of Jay Cooke and Company, a financial investment firm specializing in loans. Cooke's brother met with Secretary of the Treasury Salmon P. Chase and obtained some business for the new firm, which successfully sold some of the federal government's early war loans. Cooke also managed to sell within two weeks $3 million in loans to enable the state government to raise and equip the Pennsylvania Reserves. Then, when the government's fortunes were low after the defeat at Bull Run, Cooke wholeheartedly supported the efforts of the Treasury Department to sell three-year notes with an interest rate of 7.3 percent per year. Cooke's firm extensively advertised and promoted the government loans. He was phenomenally successful at this: In 1862, when the Treasury Department issued a new loan series called the *five-twenties* (redeem in five years, must be redeemed in twenty), Cooke was made the sole agent for their sales. By the time the series was stopped in January 1864, Cooke's firm had raised $511 million for the government.

Numerous citizens of Philadelphia organized many benevolent institutions and societies during the course of the Civil War. Two closely related such establishments were located near the Delaware River to feed incoming soldiers passing through the city. In late April 1861, a group of women wanted to help feed hungry units, so they enlisted neighborhood help. William Cooper, owner of a Southwark cooperage, donated his building to the cause and thus was born the Cooper Shop Refreshment Saloon. Located on Otsego Street just off Washington Avenue, his two-story brick building was near two railroad depots and was thus on a main route of passage of military units. Storekeepers in the area donated foodstuffs, and women from the suburbs brought in cans of milk. As the saloon enlarged its operations, the staff could feed 1,000 men an hour. The second floor of the cooperage was converted into a hospital able to bed twenty-seven patients, while the president of the Mount Moriah Cemetery donated several plots for temporary interment of deceased soldiers.

The Cooper Shop also opened a Soldiers' Home on the northwest corner of Race and Crown to house the discharged veterans and care for those who were sick or disabled. In the spring of 1865, the Cooper Shop Soldiers' Home merged with the Soldiers' Home of Philadelphia. A year later, the new organization moved into a three-story brick building, at Sixteenth Street and Filbert, that had formerly been a hospital. The home operated until 1872.

Located on Swanson Street off Washington Avenue was the Union Volunteer Refreshment Saloon, a similar venture to the Cooper. Both saloons cooperated and divided incoming soldiers among both establishments so that one would not be overwhelmed.

Philadelphia also became awash with military hospitals. At one time there were more than twenty hospitals throughout the city. The two largest eventually absorbed smaller, more temporary locations. The Satterlee United States General Hospital, located in West Philadelphia at Baltimore Avenue and Forty-fourth Street, opened for patients in June 1862 and remained in business until August 3, 1865. The hospital had a capacity of 2,860 beds, and contained a library, a reading and writing room, as well as a billiard and entertainment hall. The Chestnut Hill Hospital, officially known as the Mower United States General Hospital, was located in the Chestnut Hill section of the city. Mower at first had a bed capacity of 2,820, but this was later enlarged to 4,000. Mower opened for business on January 17, 1863. (See appendix for a list of smaller hospitals.) In fall 1863, the United States Laboratory opened in a factory building at Sixth Street and Jefferson. Here, a staff of chemists and associated experts compounded medical supplies.

Originating in New York, the United States Sanitary Commission (USSC) soon had an office in Philadelphia at 1307

Chestnut Street. Founded by the New York YMCA, the commission elected the Philadelphian George H. Steuart as chairman. The USSC supplied soldiers with clothing, books, newspapers and magazines, hospital supplies, religious tracts and bibles; its representatives aided the wounded at the front, worked in hospitals, tended to dying soldiers and helped to bury and identify the dead.

The United States Christian Commission (USCC) was similar to the USSC. The USCC also began in New York and was recognized in June 1861 by the secretary of war. Branches soon opened all over the North. Its mission was to help with the wounded both at the front and in hospitals. The commission also established a claim and pension agency, chartered and purchased hospital ships and trains, and opened forty soldiers' homes. The headquarters of the Philadelphia branch was located at 1011 Chestnut Street.

The commission organized Sanitary Fairs in major cities to raise funds to continue its work. The Great Central Fair for the Philadelphia branch took place between June 8 and June 28, 1864, in Logan Square. Huge displays included war trophies, machinery, books, clothing, hardware, photographs and much more. The fair featured a restaurant, horticultural hall, school department and art gallery. More than 440,000 admissions were recorded. President and Mrs. Lincoln visited on June 16. The fair committee reported a net profit of slightly more than $1 million.

To help maintain enthusiasm for the war effort, a group of Philadelphia businessmen met in November 1862 and established what eventually became the Union League of Philadelphia. The new organization's first home was the Kuhn Mansion at 1118 Chestnut Street. In addition to raising money to support the war, the Union League also sponsored the recruitment and equipping of nine infantry regiments as well as assisting in the formation of the state's eleven black regiments. The league also began construction of a permanent headquarters into which it moved in May 1865. The Union League still exists today in its location at 140 South Broad Street.

Overall, Philadelphia played a major role in the Civil War. The city's financial support, manpower, arsenals and shipyards, hospitals and benevolent societies all contributed to the Union's eventual success. Many of the sites are still visible today, in addition to postwar monumentation and commemoration. Come see them!

SITES CONNECTED WITH THE ABOLITION MOVEMENT AND THE UNDERGROUND RAILROAD

Philadelphia, prior to the Civil War, was a center of abolitionist activity and an active area for Underground Railroad locations. The city's black population in 1860 totaled more than 22,000—the largest of any Northern city except Baltimore. This, in addition to the Quaker influence, led to the establishment of several antislavery societies in the city. In spite of general apathy toward them, these societies and the individuals who were active in them kept the flame of freedom alive. Several sites connected with abolitionism can still be viewed today.

ABOLITION HALL, behind the intersection of the Germantown Pike and Butler Pike, Plymouth Meeting, PA.

This structure was constructed in 1858 to allow antislavery folks to have a meeting place. It also served as a station on the Underground Railroad. Built by George Corson, a Quaker and abolitionist, the hall could seat some 150 people. Abolition Hall later functioned as a studio for the artist Thomas Hovenden, who had married into the Corson family. It was there that he executed the painting *John Brown's Last Moment*.

Abolition Hall is privately owned, but the owners occasionally allow group tours. For more information, contact the Plymouth Meeting Historical Society, Box 156, Plymouth Meeting, PA 19462. Tel. 610–828–8111.

ROBERT M. ADGER HOME,
823 South Street, Philadelphia

Adger (1837–1910) was born in South Carolina and came to Philadelphia in 1848. In 1860, he organized the Fraternal Soci-

ABOLITION HALL

ABOLITION HALL

ety to help the struggle for equal rights for African Americans. During the war, Adger was a member of the Black Enlistment Committee to recruit black soldiers. He later organized the Afro-American Historical Society. After his death by heart attack in 1910, Adger was buried in Merion Cemetery.

DAVID B. BOWSER HOME, 841 N. 4th St., Philadelphia

Bowser (1820–1900) was a highly skilled black artist who began his career as a Philadelphia sign painter. Some of his most famous

ROBERT M. ADGER HOME

paintings include Abraham Lincoln and John Brown. During the war, Bowser painted regimental colors for the black regiments raised in Pennsylvania. His allegorical paintings generally portrayed blacks breaking their fetters and receiving arms or liberty.

DAVID B. BOWSER HOME

CAMPBELL AFRICAN AMERICAN METHODIST EPISCOPAL CHURCH, 1667 Kinsey Street, Philadelphia, PA 19124

Founded by Frankford blacks in 1817 in a private home, the Campbell Church (also called Second Bethel Church) was the only all-black church in the Frankford section of the city until 1869. The African Colored School held its classes here from

CAMPBELL AFRICAN AMERICAN
METHODIST EPISCOPAL CHURCH

1838 to 1840. By the 1850s, the Campbell Church was a major station on the Underground Railroad.

OCTAVIUS V. CATTO HOME,
812 South Street, Philadelphia

Catto (1839–1871) was a major of colored troops during the Civil War. He was assassinated in 1871 while rallying African-American support for the Republican Party during the 1871 elections.

JAMES FORTEN HOME,
336 Lombard Street, Philadelphia

Forten (1766–1842) was a wealthy sail maker who employed men of all races. He was a leader of the city's African-American community; in 1833, the American Anti-Slavery Society was organized in this house. A Pennsylvania Historical and Museum Commission Historical Marker can be seen outside the house.

FRANCES ELLEN WATKINS HARPER HOME,
1006 Bainbridge Street, Philadelphia

Born a free black in Baltimore, Harper (1825–1911) was forced to leave Maryland in 1853 when that state's legislature passed a law forbidding free blacks from entering the state. She came to Philadelphia, where she lectured widely in favor of the antislavery movement and became a conductor on the Underground Railroad. Harper was also a noted poet, writer and temperance reformer. Harper's home is presently a private residence and not open to the public.

JOHNSON HOUSE,
6133 Germantown Avenue, Philadelphia

Built in 1765 by the Quaker Derick Jansen for his son, John Johnson, this two-story stone house was used as an Underground Railroad station by the Johnson family. According to a written account by a family member, notables such as William Still and Harriet Tubman met in this house to discuss important antislavery matters.

Hours: April–October, Saturdays, 1 P.M. to 4 P.M.; all other times by appointment. Admission fees: $3 for adults, $1.50 for children and senior citizens. Tel. 215–438–1768.

JAMES FORTEN HOME

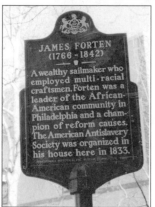

JAMES FORTEN
(1766 - 1842)

A wealthy sailmaker who employed multi-racial craftsmen, Forten was a leader of the African-American community in Philadelphia and a champion of reform causes. The American Antislavery Society was organized in his house here in 1833.

FRANCIS ELLEN WATKINS HARPER HOME

LINDEN GROVE

Directions: From I–76 (Schuylkill Expressway), exit at Lincoln Drive. Continue on Lincoln Drive through two lights. Just beyond the second light, turn onto Harvey Street and follow to its end, then turn left onto Germantown Avenue. From the Pennsylvania Turnpike, Exit 25 (Norristown). Follow the Germantown Pike east for 8 miles.

LINDEN GROVE, corner of Spring Mill Road and Ridge Pike, Plymouth Meeting, PA

Peter Dager, owner of a local marble quarry, used this structure as an Underground Railroad station quite successfully, even digging tunnels throughout the property to hide runaway slaves.

MAULSBY HOME

For information, contact the Historical Society of Montgomery County, 1654 DeKalb Street, Norristown, PA 19401. Tel. 610–272–0297.

MAULSBY HOME, intersection of Butler Pike and Germantown Pike, Plymouth Meeting, PA

Samuel Maulsby's home functioned as a major Underground Railroad station since the 1820s. Artist Thomas Hovenden lived here for several years and painted some of his antislavery works within these walls. The house is still owned by Maulsby descendants, and permission must be obtained to tour the property.

The Maulsby home is privately owned and no tours are allowed. For more information, contact the Plymouth Meeting

Historical Society, Box 156, Plymouth Meeting, PA 19462. Tel. 610–828–8111.

MOTHER BETHEL AFRICAN METHODIST EPISCOPAL CHURCH, 419 Richard Allen Avenue (Sixth Street near Lombard), Philadelphia, PA 19147

Founded in 1794, this church is better known as Mother Bethel. In 1830, Bishop Richard Allen led the first African-American convention in Philadelphia, the first such large-scale meeting dedicated to the antislavery cause. The church was a major Underground Railroad stop; such noted abolitionists as Lucretia Mott, Harriet Tubman and Frederick Douglass visited and spoke at Mother Bethel. This patch of land is the oldest real estate in America continuously owned by African Americans. The present church, built in 1889, is the fourth building on the site. A Pennsylvania Historical and Museum Commission Historical Marker is located outside the church.

Museum hours: Tuesday–Saturday, 10 A.M. to 3 P.M., or by appointment. Tel. 215–925–0616.

JAMES AND LUCRETIA MOTT RESIDENCE, Old York Road, near Beech Avenue, La Mott, PA

Nicknamed "Roadside," the home of the famous couple has disappeared, with only the gatehouse and a Pennsylvania Historical and Museum Commission Historical Marker to designate the site. The Motts occupied the house from 1857 through the war period, donating part of their land so that the government could establish Camp William Penn, which was a collection and recruiting camp for Pennsylvania's eleven black regiments. A

MOTHER BETHEL AFRICAN
METHODIST EPISCOPAL CHURCH

JAMES AND LUCRETIA MOTT RESIDENCE SITE

parade of famous Americans visited the Motts at their residence—William Lloyd Garrison, Frederick Douglass, John Greenleaf Whittier and others.

PENNSYLVANIA HALL, 6th St. and Haines, on the west side of the street, Philadelphia

The Pennsylvania Anti-Slavery Society, having trouble in finding a permanent meeting place, decided to build its own structure. This large meeting hall was erected in the years 1837–1838 and formally dedicated on May 14, 1838. Abolitionism was unpopular at this time, however, and rumors began circulating that violence was about to erupt. On May 17, the Anti-Slavery Convention of American Women was held in the hall. Other organizations also convened in Pennsylvania Hall. Mayor Swift, receiving reports that a mob was forming to disrupt the abolitionists, requested that the hall be closed. The owners complied and handed the keys to the mayor that evening. Swift ordered the mob to disperse but failed in his attempt. Although police were on the scene, a number of men with battering rams forced open the doors, piled curtains in the middle of the assembly room and started a fire that quickly engulfed the hall. The Independent Order of Odd Fellows later purchased the ruins and built a hall on the site. Today, PBS Channel 12 occupies the site of the hall. A Pennsylvania Historical and Museum Commission Historical Marker identifies the site.

WILLIAM STILL HOME,
224 S. 12th St., Philadelphia

Still (1821–1902) was born free in New Jersey and was a clerk in the Pennsylvania Anti-Slavery Society, a successful black businessman (coal and lumberyards) as well as an active Underground Railroad conductor. In 1872, he authored *The Underground Railroad*, a record of all the fugitive slaves who passed through Philadelphia's stations. His papers are included in the Blockson Collection at Temple University. Still's former home was demolished in 1992, but a Pennsylvania Historical and Museum Commission Historical Marker indicates its location.

WILLIAM WHIPPER HOUSE,
919 Lombard Street, Philadelphia

Born in Lancaster County in 1804, Whipper and his cousin became partners in a booming lumber business in the county. His home and yard became a noted stop on the Underground Railroad. By 1834, Whipper had moved to Philadelphia and continued his antislavery actions. Today, his second home is a private residence and not open to the public.

WILLIAM WHIPPER HOUSE

MUSEUMS AND LIBRARIES

AFRICAN AMERICAN MUSEUM,
701 Arch Street, Philadelphia, PA 19106

Opened in 1976, the museum was funded and built by the city. Exhibits include the history, arts, crafts, and culture of American blacks, with specialty in Pennsylvania and Philadelphia history.

Hours: Tuesday–Saturday, 10 A.M. to 5 P.M.; Sunday, noon to 6 P.M. Tel. 215–574–0380. Admission fee: $6 for adults, $4 for senior citizens, students and handicapped visitors.

Directions: The African American Museum is located two blocks west of Independence Mall and one block north of the Federal Court House and Office Building.

AMERICAN-SWEDISH HISTORICAL MUSEUM,
1900 Pattison Avenue, Philadelphia, PA 19145–5901

Located in Franklin Delano Roosevelt Park near Veterans' Stadium, this museum shows visitors the full spectrum of Swedish contribution to local and national development. Modeled after a

AFRICAN AMERICAN HISTORICAL AND CULTURAL MUSEUM

seventeenth-century Swedish manor house, the museum is located on land originally settled by Swedish colonists before William Penn came to Pennsylvania.

The prominent Civil War display pertains to John Ericsson, the inventor of the USS *Monitor*, the ironclad warship that dueled with CSS *Virginia* in the first battle of ironclad warships in 1862. The library contains one of the two largest collections of Ericsson's personal papers. Also of interest is a collection of memorabilia relating to Jenny Lind, the famous opera singer nicknamed the "Swedish Nightingale." She toured America before the war; this collection commemorates her successful visit. Fredrika Bremer, Swedish novelist and advocate for women's and human rights, visited America in the years 1849–50 and was

AMERICAN-SWEDISH HISTORICAL MUSEUM

stirred to write novels for social change. Exhibits and a room named in her honor showcase her accomplishments.

Hours: Tuesday–Friday, 10 A.M. to 4 P.M.; Saturday and Sunday, noon to 4 P.M.; closed Mondays and holidays. Tel. 215–389–1776. Web site: www.americanswedish.org. Admission fee: $6 for adults, $5 for seniors and students with ID, children

AMERICAN-SWEDISH HISTORICAL MUSEUM

age 12 to 18, and free for children under 12 accompanied by an adult.

Directions: Located near the Philadelphia sports complex, the museum is easily accessible from both I–95 and I–76 and has plenty of free parking. The Broad Street subway is within walking distance; the no. 17 bus brings you directly to the museum.

CHARLES L. BLOCKSON AFRO-AMERICAN COLLECTION, Sullivan Hall, first floor, Temple University, Twelfth Street and Berks Mall, Philadelphia, PA 19122

The Blockson Collection is one of the outstanding research centers devoted to the African-American experience in the world. More than 40,000 items include 25,000 books, 3,500 rare books and 15,000 pamphlets, slave narratives, letters, posters, recordings, sheet music and statues. Special collections include the John Brown Collection, a variety of memorabilia on Brown's life as well as the Abolition Society of Pennsylvania; the African and Afro-American Slave Narrative Collection, more than 100 narratives that include works of Frederick Douglass, Sojourner Truth and Venture Smith; the Underground Railroad Collection, from Blockson's personal efforts (one of the largest in the country), including the papers of William Still; and the John Mosley Photograph Collection, a 1985 addition of some 500,000 prints and negatives.

Material in the Blockson Collection does not circulate and must be used on site; photocopying and photography services are available.

Hours: Monday–Friday, 9 A.M. to 5 P.M. Closed during regular holidays and some university academic calendar breaks. Tel. 215–787–6632. Web site: www.library.temple.edu/blockson. Admission fee: Free.

Directions: Temple University can be reached by traveling north on Broad Street from center city.

CHESTNUT HILL HISTORICAL SOCIETY,
8708 Germantown Avenue, Philadelphia, PA 19118

This historical society includes a current exhibit on the Chestnut Hill Hospital, also known as Mower General Hospital, the largest wartime military hospital in the city. The society also has a large file of information gathered to document the plaque that marks the hospital site. Due to a small staff, it is recommended that visitors who wish to use the archives call ahead for reservations.

Hours: Monday–Friday, 9 A.M. to 5 P.M. Tel. 215–247–0417. Admission fee: Free to members, nominal fee for non-members.

THE CIVIL WAR LIBRARY AND MUSEUM,
1805 Pine Street, Philadelphia, PA 19101

This library and museum was one of the city's best-kept secrets until recent years, when the establishment began advertising more often and instituted a series of changing exhibits. Founded in 1888, the library was that of the Military Order of the Loyal Legion of the United States (MOLLUS), a Union veterans' group organized in 1865. Its membership was restricted to officers who had served honorably in the Union army and navy. MOLLUS continues today with descendants of Union officers.

The red brick rowhouse at 1805 Pine Street is crowded with books and memorabilia, all devoted to the Civil War. The library consists of more than 16,000 volumes, including regimental histories, general war histories, biographies, battle and campaign studies and pictorial studies. Also housed within the structure are more than 2,000 photographs of soldiers and wartime scenes as well as a number of manuscript collections. Prominent among the library's holdings are the papers of Frank A. Donaldson (118th PA), St. Clair A. Mulholland (116th PA), Francis A. Walker (Second Army Corps officer and historian) and William J. Bolton (51st PA).

The museum holdings are spectacular. Major General George G. Meade's dress uniform and presentation swords are on display, as are his headquarters flags. A room devoted to Abraham Lincoln contains several busts of the martyred chief executive, an original playbill from Ford's Theater, shreds of bunting from the flag that decorated Lincoln's theater box, life-size casts of Lincoln's face and hands, as well as many other artifacts. Throughout the several rooms and floors of the museum, visitors can see different types of firearms and swords, drums, souvenired pieces of wood with bullets embedded in them, musical instruments, mess kits and flags. An upstairs room is furnished as a Victorian

THE CIVIL WAR LIBRARY AND MUSEUM

THE CIVIL WAR LIBRARY AND MUSEUM

THE CIVIL WAR LIBRARY AND MUSEUM

parlor, complete with harpsichord and John Philip Sousa marches on the music stand. Another room is devoted to the Union navy and features a handmade model of USS *Monitor*.

In recent years, the museum has refurbished two first-floor rooms for alternating exhibits. Recent topics included women's period clothing, prisoners and prisons, black soldiers, and blockade runners. There is also a small museum shop. The Old Baldy Civil War Round Table uses the library as its meeting place on the second Thursday of every month.

Hours: Thursday–Saturday, 11 A.M. to 4:30 P.M. Tel. 215–735–8196. Web site: www.libertynet.org/cwlm. Admission fee: $5 for adults, $4 for senior citizens, $3 for students, children under 12 free.

Directions: The Civil War Library and Museum is located south of Rittenhouse Square in a residential neighborhood, where parking is at a premium. The closest off-street parking lot is at the corner of Pine and Seventeenth Streets.

COLLEGE OF PHYSICIANS LIBRARY,
19 S. 22nd Street, Philadelphia, PA 19103

The College of Physicians is the nation's oldest medical society, founded in 1787. In addition to an interesting medical museum, the college maintains a comprehensive library. Among the rare book holdings are a history of Satterlee General Hospital, numerous reminiscences of surgeons and hospital workers, manuals and reports. The Manuscripts Department includes the following collections.

☞ Bartoll, William H. Diary, January–June 1864. Naval surgeon

- ☞ Broad Street Hospital, Cherry Street Branch. Ward C Medical Case-book
- ☞ Cruice, John J. Papers. Surgeon
- ☞ Cruice, Robert B. Papers. Surgeon
- ☞ Gross, Samuel W. Letter and Order Book, First Kentucky Brigade, USA
- ☞ Mintzer, John W. Papers. Surgeon
- ☞ Mitchell, S. Weir. Turner's Lane Hospital Cases and Studies
- ☞ Norris, William F. Papers. Surgeon

The library also contains the *West Philadelphia Hospital Register* and *The Haversack*, one of the many publications of the June 1864 Sanitary Commission Fair.

Hours: Tuesday–Friday, 10 A.M. to 4 P.M., by appointment only. Tel. 215–563–3737. Web site: www.collphyphil.org.

Directions: From the Schuylkill Expressway, exit at John F. Kennedy Boulevard. At Nineteenth Street, turn south and then right (west) on Sansom to Twenty-second, then north (right) on Twenty-second.

FIRST TROOP PHILADELPHIA CITY CAVALRY MUSEUM, The Armory, Twenty-third and Ranstead Streets, Philadelphia, PA 19103

The First Troop, Philadelphia City Cavalry is the nation's oldest military unit in continuous service. It was formed in 1774 and has served the country in numerous wars ever since. During the Civil War, the First City Troop immediately volunteered for three-month duty in 1861, then again as volunteer militia during the Gettysburg campaign. Throughout the war, many of the troop's 1861 members served with distinction in other units; two

FIRST TROOP PHILADELPHIA CITY CAVALRY MUSEUM

outstanding examples were Colonel Thomas C. James and Colonel R. Butler Price, both of the 2nd Pennsylvania Cavalry. The unit also carries the lineage for the 6th Pennsylvania Cavalry (Rush's Lancers).

Construction for the present armory building began in 1900 after a heavy snow collapsed the roof of the previous armory. The museum is open by prior appointment, and the unit maintains an archives and library. Museum holdings include weapons, uniforms, silver sets, photographs, paintings and flags, all pertaining to the history of the troop from its beginning in 1774 to the present. Today the unit is part of the Pennsylvania Army National Guard—Troop A, 1st Squadron, 104th Cavalry, 28th Division (Mechanized).

Hours: By appointment only. Tel. 215–564–1488.

Directions: The First City Troop Armory is located near the east bank of the Schuylkill River, one block from the College of Physicians.

FREE LIBRARY OF PHILADELPHIA,
1901 Vine Street, Philadelphia

Built in 1891, this library contains more than six million items, including an excellent rare books room, a large area newspaper collection and other specialized collections. Researchers seeking 1860s newspapers can find a number of titles on microfilm, including the *Daily Evening Bulletin*, *Inquirer*, *Press* and *Public Ledger*.

The *Weekly Times* can also be found here. This weekly version of the daily *Times* began in 1877 and centered around contributions by Civil War veterans called "Annals of the War." Publisher Alexander K. McClure printed a book containing more than 100 of the early articles in 1879, but this important series finally ceased in the late 1880s after more than 1,000 articles

FIRST TROOP PHILADELPHIA CITY CAVALRY MUSEUM

appeared in the paper. The Free Library may be the only library in the country with a fairly complete run of this paper.

The Free Library also has the Philadelphia *Weekly Press*. Owned by Isaac Pennypacker, the weekly version of the *Press* carried the series "Pennsylvania in the War," which ran from 1886 to 1889, and contained articles by Union and Confederate veterans.

Hours: Monday–Wednesday, 9 A.M. to 9 P.M.; Thursday–Friday, 9 A.M. to 6 P.M.; Saturday, 9 A.M. to 5 P.M.; Sunday, 1 P.M. to 5 P.M.; closed holidays and on Sundays during the summer. Tel. 215–567–2282. Web site: www.library.phila.gov.

Directions: The Free Library is just north of Logan Circle.

GRAND ARMY OF THE REPUBLIC CIVIL WAR MUSEUM AND LIBRARY, 4278 Griscom Street, Philadelphia, PA 19124

The Grand Army of the Republic (GAR) was the largest Union veterans' organization founded after the Civil War. At its peak in the 1880s, the GAR numbered almost 500,000 members, organized into posts scattered across the country. Philadelphia boasted several dozen such posts, including the prestigious Post 2, which occupied a structure formerly located on N. 12th St. In 1958, this area of the city was rebuilt and the post, now run by the Sons of Union Veterans, was forced to vacate. The Sons purchased the present house shortly thereafter. Dating from 1796, the current GAR building was constructed by Dr. John Ruan as his residence.

The museum houses the remaining artifacts and library of Post 2 as well as several smaller GAR posts from around the city. Relics include remnants of battleflags, a piece of the pillow on which Abraham Lincoln died, a pair of wood-soled Confederate shoes from the Gettysburg battlefield, a uniform of the 72nd Pennsylvania (Baxter's Fire Zouaves), weapons, ammunition, personal effects of soldiers and more. The library contains more than 3,000 volumes, including several GAR post record books.

The table on pages 46–47 lists the GAR posts in the city. Each state's GAR posts were numbered consecutively, reflecting the order in which the posts were formed.

Hours: Third Monday of every month, 7 P.M. to 9 P.M.; second Tuesday of every month, 7 P.M. to 9 P.M.; first Sunday of every month, noon to 5 P.M.; Tuesday and Wednesday, 10 A.M. to 2 P.M.; and by appointment. Tel. 215–289–6484. Web site: www.suvcw.org/garmus.htm. Admission fee: Free, but donations are gladly accepted.

Post	Location
Gen. George G. Meade Post 1	*Parkway Building, Broad and Cherry Streets*
Post 2	*667–669 N. 12th St.*
Gen. U. S. Grant Post 5	*1706 South Street*
Ellis Post 6	*Germantown Town Hall*
Capt. William S. Newhall Post 7	*Girard Avenue and Eyre Street*
Gen. E. D. Baker Post 8	*1417 Columbia Avenue*
Lieut. John T. Greble Post 10	*721 Wharton Street*
Hetty A. Jones Post 12	*Roxborough*
Col. Ulric Dahlgren Post 14	*2434 Kensington Avenue*
Gen. G. K. Warren Post 15	*Carson Street, Manayunk*
Col. William L. Curry Post 18	*317 N. 20th St.*
Col. Fred Taylor Post 19	*1431 Brown Street*
Courtland Saunders Post 21	*39th St. above Market Street*
Admiral DuPont Post 24	*Broad and Federal Streets*
John W. Jackson Post 27	*409 S. 11th St.*
The Cavalry Post 35	*Parkway Building, Broad and Cherry Streets*
Gen. Gustavus W. Town Post 46	*1421 South Street*
Philip R. Schuyler Post 51	*Sepviva and Norris Streets*
Gen. Phil Kearny Post 55	*4604 Frankford Avenue*

Post	Location
Col. John W. Moore Post 56	*3930 Lancaster Avenue*
Gen. D. B. Birney Post 63	*Germantown Avenue and Diamond Street*
Gen. John F. Reynolds Post 71	*1226 S. 8th St.*
Post 77	*524 N. 6th St.*
George Smith Post 79	*Conshohocken*
Robert Bryan Post 80	*11th and Fitzwater Streets*
Anna M. Ross Post 94	*Girard Avenue and Hutchinson Street*
Charles Sumner Post 103	*1224 N. 11th St.*
Winfield Scott Post 114	*2054 Ridge Avenue*
Gen. John A. Logan Post 115	*1231 S. 17th St.*
Hector Tyndale Post 160	*1365 Ridge Avenue*
Pennsylvania Reserve Post 191	*5th and Chestnut Streets*
J. A. Koltes Post 228	*236–38 George Street*
Gen. Robert Patterson Post 275	*1131 S. Broad Street*
Lieut. E. W. Gay Post 312	*2214 Germantown Avenue*
Col. James Ashworth Post 334	*Frankford Avenue*
Gen. Thomas C. Devin Post 363	*Parkway Building, Broad and Cherry Streets*
The Naval Post 400	*132 S. 8th St.*

GRAND ARMY OF THE REPUBLIC CIVIL WAR MUSEUM

MUSEUMS AND LIBRARIES ❧ 49

Directions: The GAR Museum and Library is located in the Frankford section of the city. From I–95, exit at Bridge Street, west to Frankford Avenue, then left through eight traffic lights to Church Street. Turn right and follow to Griscom. Turn left: Ruan House is at the end of the block on the right. Parking is available behind the museum or at the church on the corner of Church and Griscom. From Roosevelt Boulevard, exit at Oxford Avenue (Route 232). Travel east on Oxford to Griscom Street. Turn right on Griscom: the GAR building is on the right at the end of seven blocks.

HISTORICAL SOCIETY OF FRANKFORD,
1507 Orthodox Street, Philadelphia, PA 19124

This small historical society preserves the heritage of Frankford and Northeast Philadelphia. Among its holdings are Civil War artifacts and the Lodge Collection, which contains works on Lincoln and the Civil War.

Hours: For researchers, by appointment only. Tel. 215–743–6030.

HISTORICAL SOCIETY OF PENNSYLVANIA,
1300 Locust Street, Philadelphia, PA 19107

The Historical Society is one of the nation's foremost special collections facilities. The library collection numbers at least fifteen million items, including letters, diaries, newspapers, photographs and other material.

The Civil War holdings include numerous manuscript collections. High points of interest are the papers of Major General George G. Meade, commander of the Army of the Potomac; Major General Andrew A. Humphreys, Army of the Potomac division leader and later commander of the Second Army Corps;

HISTORICAL SOCIETY OF PENNSYLVANIA

Brigadier General George A. McCall, commander of the Pennsylvania Reserves; and Major General John Gibbon, Union division and corps commander.

Other outstanding collections include the papers of William F. Biddle (aide to Major General George B. McClellan), Cecil

HISTORICAL SOCIETY OF PENNSYLVANIA

Clay (58th Pennsylvania), GAR Post 51 Papers and Books, Thomas J. Jordan (9th Pennsylvania Cavalry), John L. Smith (118th Pennsylvania), William B. Rawle (3rd Pennsylvania Cavalry) and the Union Volunteer Refreshment Saloon Papers.

For more complete information on the Historical Society's collections and Civil War manuscripts, see *Guide to the Manuscript Collections of the Historical Society of Pennsylvania*, published by the society in 1991, or visit the web site. See also the appendix herein, which lists the primary Civil War collections available for research at the Historical Society of Pennsylvania.

Hours: Tuesday, Thursday, Friday, 9:30 A.M. to 4:45 P.M.; Wednesday, 1 P.M. to 8:45 P.M.; Saturday, 10 A.M. to 4:45 P.M. Tel. 215–732–6201. Web site: www.hsp.org. Admission fee: $6 for

INDEPENDENCE SEAPORT MUSEUM

nonmembers; $3 for students age 14 and over; no visitors under age 14 admitted.

INDEPENDENCE SEAPORT MUSEUM,
211 South Columbus Boulevard, Philadelphia, PA 19106

This excellent maritime museum has a number of archival collections that cover the shipbuilders located in and around the city. One of the museum's permanent exhibits chronicles the history of the Philadelphia Navy Yard.

Hours: Open seven days a week, 10 A.M. to 5 P.M. Tel. 215–925–5439. Web site: www.phillyseaport.org. Admission fee: $8 for adults, $6.50 for senior citizens, $4 for children age 5 to 12, children under 5 admitted free. Admission is free on Sundays from 10 A.M. to noon. Admission fee includes USS *Olympia* (Admiral Dewey's flagship in 1898) and USS *Becuna* (a World War II submarine).

LIBRARY COMPANY OF PHILADELPHIA,
1314 Locust Street, Philadelphia, PA 19107

Founded in 1731, the Library Company is the oldest public library in the country and the only colonial-era library to survive virtually intact. Its 500,000-volume collection includes over 75,000 graphics, 160,000 manuscripts and many rare books. Of interest to Civil War researchers is the company's outstanding collection of area recruiting broadsides and posters. The collections also include lithographs, watercolors, and photographs of wartime Philadelphia and its military facilities as well as the scrapbook collection of John McAllister.

Hours: Monday–Friday, 9 A.M. to 4:45 P.M. Tel. 215–546–3181. Web site: www.librarycompany.org. Admission fee: Free.

Directions: The Library Company is located in the same block as the Historical Society of Pennsylvania.

NATIONAL ARCHIVES,
Mid Atlantic Region, GSA Regional Office Building,
900 Market Street, Room 1350, Philadelphia, PA 19107

The Mid Atlantic Regional Branch of the National Archives contains much of interest to Civil War researchers. National Archives records are divided into Record Groups, each of which pertains to

LIBRARY COMPANY OF PHILADELPHIA

a single federal agency. The following Record Groups include Civil War records.

☞ Record Group 21, Records of the U.S. District Courts, contains files for the states of Delaware, Pennsylvania, Maryland, Virginia and West Virginia, as well as some Confederate records for Virginia

☞ Record Group 24, Records of the Bureau of Naval Personnel, includes material on the Naval Home and Naval Hospital

☞ Record Group 52, Records of the Bureau of Medicine and Surgery, includes material from the U.S. Naval Asylum

☞ Record Group 71, Records of the Bureau of Yards and Docks, has information about the U.S. Naval Asylum and the Naval Home

☞ Record Group 77, Records of the Office of the Chief of Engineers, includes material on the Baltimore and Philadelphia Districts

☞ Record Group 79, Records of the National Park Service, includes material on several Civil War–related parks, including Antietam and Gettysburg

☞ Record Group 92, Records of the Office of the Quartermaster General, include records of the Philadelphia Depot and Schyulkill Arsenal

☞ Record Group 127, Records of the U.S. Marine Corps, has material from the Philadelphia and Norfolk barracks

☞ Record Group 156, Records of the Office of the Chief of Ordnance, includes material on the Frankford Arsenal, the Allegheny Arsenal (Pittsburgh) and the Fort Monroe Arsenal

☞ Record Group 181, Records of Naval Districts and Shore Establishments, contains records of the Philadelphia and Norfolk Navy Yards

Guides to the branch holdings in general and the Civil War in particular are available upon request.

Hours: Monday–Friday, 8 A.M. to 5 P.M.; on the second and fourth Saturdays of every month, 8 A.M. to 4 P.M. Tel. 215–597–3000. Web site: www.nara.gov. Admission fee: Free.

Directions: The National Archives branch is four blocks west of Independence Mall, in the federal building, so parking is very hard to find in the area. Perhaps it is best to park your car underground at Independence Mall and walk the distance.

NATIONAL MUSEUM OF AMERICAN JEWISH HISTORY, Independence Mall East, 55 N. 5th St., Philadelphia, PA 19106

More than 10,000 Jewish Americans served in the Civil War: 7,000 for the Union armies, and 3,000 in the Confederate armies. The museum's permanent exhibit "Creating American Jews" features a section on participation in the Civil War.

Hours: Monday–Thursday, 10 A.M. to 5 P.M.; Friday, 10 A.M. to 3 P.M.; Sunday, noon to 5 P.M. Tel. 215–923–3811. Web site: www.nmajh.org. Admission fee: $3 for adults, $2 for senior citizens, students and children over 6, and children under 6 admitted free.

Directions: The National Museum of American Jewish History is east of Independence Mall, two blocks south of the United States Mint and convenient to underground parking at the mall.

103RD ENGINEER BATTALION ARMORY, Thirty-third Street and Lancaster Avenue, Philadelphia, PA 19103

The 103rd Engineer Battalion, a unit of the Pennsylvania National Guard, traces its lineage to the years preceding the Civil War. During the war itself, the 118th and 119th Pennsylvania Volunteer Infantry regiments both were a part of the 103rd's heritage. The engineer battalion's museum in its armory building includes a number of artifacts from both the 118th and 119th.

Hours: By appointment only. Tel. 215–823–4850.

Directions: Located in west Philadelphia, the armory can be reached by exiting the Schuylkill Expressway at John F. Kennedy Boulevard and traveling west around the Thirtieth Street Station to

Thirty-third Street. Turn right (north on Thirty-third Street): the armory is in the first block.

PENNSYLVANIA ACADEMY OF FINE ARTS, Museum of American Art, 118 N. Broad Street, Philadelphia

The Pennsylvania Academy of Fine Arts is the nation's oldest art school, founded in 1805; the museum opened in 1876 and was extensively renovated a century later. Designed by the noted architect Frank Furness, the museum building's Victorian Gothic style is alone worth the visit. As its name suggests, the museum collects American artwork; its collection numbers more than 1,700 paintings, 300 sculptures and more than 14,000 works on paper. The museum indeed has some paintings that depict Civil War scenes. Since the collection's finding aid is organized by artist, it is helpful to know in advance what you are looking for, especially considering that much of the collection is in storage and prior appointments must be made for examining items not on display. Among the artists represented is William Trego, whose later nineteenth-century battle scenes were acclaimed for their realism. The museum also has Xanthus Smith's *Final Assault on Fort Fisher, North Carolina*.

Hours: Tuesday–Saturday, 10 A.M. to 5 P.M.; Sunday, 11 A.M. to 5 P.M. Tel. 215–972–7600. Admission fee: $5 for adults, $4 for senior citizens and students, $3 for children age 5 to 18.

PHILADELPHIA CITY ARCHIVES, 3101 Market Street, first floor, Philadelphia, PA 19104

For researchers looking for official information on the history of Philadelphia, this is the place to start. In addition to vital statistics such as births, deaths, marriages and real estate transactions, the city archives include city council proceedings, records of the mayor's office, military enrollment books, and photographs.

Hours: Monday–Friday, 8:30 A.M. to 5 P.M. Tel. 215–686–1776. Admission fee: Free.

UNION LEAGUE OF PHILADELPHIA,
140 S. Broad Street, Philadelphia, PA 19102

Organized in 1862, the Union League of Philadelphia is the oldest Republican club organization in the country. During the Civil War, the league supported the raising of troops in the city, helping to arm and equip several local regiments. These Pennsylvania infantry units included the 45th Militia (1st Union League), 52nd Militia (2nd Union League), 59th Militia (3rd Union

UNION LEAGUE OF PHILADELPHIA

UNION LEAGUE OF PHILADELPHIA

League), 183rd (4th Union League), 196th (5th Union League), 198th (6th Union League), 213th (7th Union League), 214th (8th Union League) and 215th (9th Union League). In addition, the league also assisted with the formation of the state's eleven black regiments at Camp William Penn. The Union League's headquarters was originally at 1118 Chestnut Street; on May 11, 1865, the organization moved into its present building on Broad Street.

In addition to maintaining the historical records of the Union League, the league also contains a fine Civil War library, including many regimental histories, Lincoln biographies and general Civil War histories. The building also houses a fine oil portrait collection as well as several war-related paintings, including two famous naval scenes by Xanthus Smith, one showing the *Monitor–Merrimac* duel, the other showing the engagement

UNION LEAGUE OF PHILADELPHIA

between *Kearsarge* and *Alabama*. Outside the Broad Street entrance is a life-size bronze statue of a Union soldier of the "Gray Reserves" by the famed sculptor H. K. Bush-Brown. The league also has several guest rooms available for rent for scholars and researchers; call ahead for reservations and availability.

The Union League building is a fine example of the new Second Empire architectural style inspired by the building proclivities of Napoleon III's revived French empire. Designed by John Fraser, the building's construction began in 1864. The brick and brownstone building is one of a very few structures erected in the city during the war. It has a mansard roof, with a monumental staircase fronting on Broad Street. A number of additions were erected in the rear of the building lot; the existing building was completed in the years 1909–1911. The building once had ornamental iron roof trim and an asymmetrical tower that was removed in the 1920s.

Hours: By appointment only. Tel. 215–563–6500; library, 215–587–5594; archives, 215–587–5592. Web site: www.union league.org.

Directions: The Union League is two blocks south of City Hall on Broad Street.

WAGNER FREE INSTITUTE OF SCIENCE,
1700 W. Montgomery Avenue, Philadelphia, PA 19121

This museum is included in this guidebook because the Wagner exemplifies the appearance of a nineteenth-century museum. William Wagner, prominent Philadelphia merchant and collector of natural history specimens, was the driving force behind this museum. The building was completed in 1865 and contains a huge exhibition hall with more than 21,000 specimens, ranging from mollusks and dinosaur bones to minerals, birds and fish. A Discovery Room allows children to handle selected items. The building is a national historic landmark.

Hours: Tuesday–Friday, 9 A.M. to 4 P.M. Tel. 215–763–6529. Web site: www.libertynet.org/wagner. Admission fee: Free, with 50¢ charge for the Discovery Room.

WAGNER FREE INSTITUTE OF SCIENCE

Directions: From both I–76 and I–95, take 676 (Vine Street Expressway) to the Broad Street exit. Take Broad Street north to Norris Street (you'll see Temple University banners on the right in this area). Turn left on Norris, go three blocks to Seventeenth Street, then make a left and follow Seventeenth Street one block to Montgomery Avenue.

╾─━▶ **4** ◀━─╼

CIVIL WAR SITES

CAMP WILLIAM PENN,
7322 Sycamore Avenue, La Mott, PA

Located in Cheltenham Township, just north of the present city limits, Camp William Penn was established in mid-1863 as a training camp for black regiments raised within the state. James and Lucretia Mott, a husband and wife team of fervent Quaker abolitionists, owned large tracts of land here and donated part of their farm to establish the camp. Eventually, eleven regiments of United States Colored Troops (the 3rd, 6th, 8th, 22nd, 24th, 25th, 32nd, 41st, 43rd, 45th, and 127th) were formed here and went off to war. Totaling more than 10,000 officers and men, these units sustained 1,056 casualties.

Lieutenant Colonel Louis Wagner of the 88th Pennsylvania, badly wounded at Second Manassas, was placed in command of the camp. A committee formed in the city to recruit black men for the new regiments. Located only half a mile from the Chel-

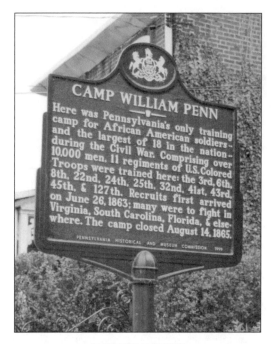

CAMP WILLIAM PENN

ten Hills depot of the North Pennsylvania Railroad, Camp William Penn was built near a stream for water, and featured a wonderful view of the rural countryside around the camp. The soldiers at first slept in the regulation army shelter tents. By year's end, wooden barracks and a host of other buildings had been constructed. The camp remained active until May 1865, when the last troops departed.

The property then reverted to the family. Lucretia Mott, demonstrating her genuine concern for the black man, donated at that time a large tract of the property for the creation of the

CAMP WILLIAM PENN

first integrated residential community in the United States. It was first called Camptown, and later changed to La Mott. The first six houses built in the town were constructed from lumber salvaged from Camp William Penn's barracks.

Today, the only remaining vestige of Camp William Penn is its entrance gate, located at 7322 Sycamore Avenue. Area residents, led by Perry Triplett, are in the process of attempting to secure funding to build a museum that honors the military participation of black Americans in wars from colonial times to the present.

Directions: From center city, take Broad Street (Route 611) north to Cheltenham Avenue. Turn left on Cheltenham, then right on Sycamore (the third street after turning onto Cheltenham). From the Pennsylvania Turnpike, take Exit 27 (Willow Grove), then take Route 611 (Old York Road) south to Cheltenham Avenue; turn left on Cheltenham, then left on Sycamore. As you near Sycamore, the La Mott Historic District is on your right.

CITY HALL, Broad and Market Streets, Philadelphia, PA 19104

This huge Italianate building, one of the largest municipal buildings in the world, was begun in 1871 and not finished until after the turn of that century. The best-known architectural symbol of Philadelphia is the 37-foot statue of William Penn perched atop the building's central tower, rising some 548 feet above the streets. Penn's statue was the city's highest point until the construction in recent years of skyscrapers in center city. Equestrian statues of Major Generals John F. Reynolds (north front) and George B. McClellan (northwest side) can be seen at street level. The bronze statue of Matthias W. Baldwin, founder of the Baldwin Locomotive Works, is also on City Hall Plaza. A bronze statue of President William McKinley is located on the south side of the hall. McKinley served with the 23rd Ohio and was cited for bravery at Antietam.

Hours: Monday–Friday, 9 A.M. to 5 P.M.; guided tours are given at 12:30 P.M. each day; call 215–568–3351 for more information. Tel. 215–686–1776 (general number).

CLARK PARK (Satterlee U.S. General Hospital Site)

One of the largest military hospitals in the Philadelphia area was originally called the West Philadelphia General Hospital. It opened for patients in June 1862. A year later, its name was changed to the Satterlee U.S. General Hospital, in honor of Brigadier General Richard S. Satterlee, a New York surgeon who was Medical Purveyor. The hospital consisted of a two-story

CLARK PARK

administration building and thirty-four single-story wards, all built of wood. Its full capacity was 2,860 beds, with tents erected on the parade ground outside the stockade providing shelter for another 900 patients. Satterlee was in operation until August 3, 1865. Soon after, the site was purchased and divided into building lots under the name Satterlee Heights.

Today, nothing remains of the actual hospital site, which extended from Baltimore Avenue to Pine Street, and from Forty-third to Forty-sixth Streets. The southeastern tip of the site is now located within the north edge of Clark Park, located just south of Baltimore Avenue between Forty-third and Forty-fourth Streets. In 1916, veterans placed a stone from the Gettysburg battlefield in the park to commemorate Satterlee Hospital; a plaque describing the hospital rests at the base of this stone.

Hours: Daily during daylight hours. Admission fee: None.

Directions: From I–76, exit on University Avenue. Proceed on University Ave. three blocks to Baltimore Avenue (PA Route 13). Turn left on Baltimore Ave.: Clark Park is on the left between Forty-third and Forty-fourth Streets.

1800 BLOCK OF DELANCEY PLACE

Delancey Place was opened in 1853 to accommodate the westward expansion of the city and the more well-to-do families who moved into the western edge of the developing city. The 1800 block of the street saw the northside houses largely finished by 1860, with the southern side done by 1880. Houses were built in the Italianate style, with later additions and alterations giving the street a more Victorian appearance. Visitors strolling along this block can catch a glimpse of upper-class Philadelphia as it appeared on the eve of war. Major General George G. Meade lived at no. 1836, and died there on November 6, 1870; a Penn-

1800 BLOCK OF DELANCEY PLACE

sylvania Historical and Museum Commission sign is located outside the building.

Directions: Delancey Place is only a brief walk north one block from the Civil War Library and Museum at 1805 Pine Street.

1800 BLOCK OF DELANCEY PLACE

EBENEZER MAXWELL MANSION,
200 West Tulpehocken Street, Philadelphia, PA 19144

Built in 1859, this fine museum offers a rare glimpse of life in a rising middle-class home between 1860 and 1880. The stone house was constructed in the eclectic Victorian style, including Second Empire and Gothic elements. The mansion, located on a street in Germantown, was intended by Maxwell to combine the best of both urban and rural living. The first floor has been restored to the 1860s period and includes a formal dining room,

EBENEZER MAXWELL MANSION

parlor and kitchen. The second floor is being restored to the period after 1876. The mansion's original iron fence encloses Victorian period gardens.

Hours: April–December, Friday–Sunday, 1 P.M. to 4 P.M. Group tours may also be arranged for all other times. Tel. 215–438–1861. Admission fee: $4 for adults, $3 for seniors and groups, $2 for students.

EBENEZER MAXWELL MANSION

FAIRMOUNT PARK, ADMINISTRATIVE OFFICES,
Memorial Hall, P.O. Box 21601, Philadelphia, PA 19131

Christened "Faire Mount" by William Penn, today's Fairmount Park, which covers some 8,700 acres, is the largest green space in any American city. In the later eighteenth and early nineteenth centuries, a number of prominent families built expensive mansions in the area. The site of the current park, straddling the Schuylkill River, was heavily forested when discovered by European explorers. By 1815, the high ground above the river included the new Fairmount Water Works, the first large-scale water purification system in America.

Beginning in 1836, the city began to purchase some of these estates when they went up for sale. This trend increased in the 1850s as more estates came within city jurisdiction. In 1867, the state legislature empowered the city to purchase additional land so that Fairmount Park could be maintained forever as an open public place. A park commission was also established that year, and in 1872, the Fairmount Park Art Commission was created to oversee the erection of suitable outdoor statues. The New World's first Zoological Gardens opened in 1874. Two years later, the park hosted the nation's Centennial International Exposition with the erection of ninety buildings for this "world's fair." Today, only Memorial Hall remains of the major buildings. (Memorial Hall is open Monday–Friday, 8:30 A.M. to 5 P.M.)

Over the years, additional work increased the size of the park and made it more accessible to center city. The Benjamin Franklin Parkway, finished in 1937, linked center city with the park. The Philadelphia Museum of Art, begun in 1919 and opened to the public almost a decade later, dominates the northwestern terminus of the parkway.

Civil War–related statuary in the park includes the following.

Army and Navy Pylons, erected in 1927, can be seen on the Parkway at Twentieth Street and Vine, diagonally across from the Free Library. These obelisks commemorate the city's Civil War dead. The sculptor was Herman A. MacNeil.

James A. Garfield bronze portrait bust and symbolic figure by the famed sculptor August St. Gaudens, located on East River

ARMY AND NAVY PYLONS STATUE

Drive. It was erected in 1896 by the Fairmount Park Art Association.

Ulysses S. Grant equestrian statue, at Fountain Green Drive. Modeled by Daniel C. French and Edward C. Potter. Erected by the Fairmount Park Art Association in 1899, on the seventy-seventh anniversary of Grant's birth. President William McKinley was among the invited guests.

ARMY AND NAVY PYLONS STATUE

Abraham Lincoln, bronze seated figure holding a copy of the Emancipation Proclamation, located on East River Drive at the Sedgley Avenue intersection. Sculpted by Randolph Rogers and unveiled in 1871, the gift of the Lincoln Monument Association. Lincoln, appropriately, faces south.

Major General George G. Meade bronze equestrian statue, located on Lansdowne Drive. Sculpted by Alexander M. Calder and erected in 1887 by the Fairmount Park Art Association. The

ARMY AND NAVY PYLONS STATUE

statue is located on the north side of Memorial Hall, within sight of Smith Memorial Arch.

All Wars Memorial to Colored Soldiers and Sailors Monument, presently located on the Parkway at Twentieth Street, at Logan Circle. The original position was on Landsdowne Drive; the memorial was moved in 1994 to its present, more visible

GEN. ULYSSES S. GRANT EQUESTRIAN STATUE

ALL WARS MEMORIAL TO COLORED SOLDIERS STATUE

SOLDIERS MONUMENT STATUE   GALUSHA PENNYPACKER STATUE

location. Sculpted by J. Otto Schweiger to honor the participation of black Americans in the Civil War.

Soldiers Monument, on Belmont Avenue near the intersection with Montgomery Drive. Sculpted by McNeil Corey. This monument was one of hundreds erected all over the North by Grand Army of the Republic posts after the war.

Galusha Pennypacker, sculpted by Albert Laessle in 1934. Located on the northeast side of the intersection of the Benjamin Franklin Parkway at Nineteenth Street.

Smith Memorial Arch, northwest and southwest corners of North Concourse and Lansdowne Drive, located near the Memorial Hall. This gigantic granite arch, erected between 1897 and 1912, was the gift of foundry owner Richard Smith, and is

SMITH MEMORIAL ARCH

an inspiring expression of late nineteenth century patriotism. The architect James H. Windrim designed the arch in the Italian Renaissance style. Bronze standing statues of Major Generals George G. Meade and John F. Reynolds adorn the monument, while bronze equestrian statues of Major Generals George B. McClellan and Winfield S. Hancock can also be seen. Eight colossal busts include Admiral David D. Porter, Major General John F. Hartranft, Admiral John F. Dahlgren, Major General Samuel W. Crawford, Governor Andrew G. Curtin, and Brigadier General James A. Beaver. The frieze is carved with the names of eighty-four Pennsylvanians of note who participated in the Civil War. In the rear of the memorial is the famous Whispering Wall. A curved bench along the wall transmits a whisper from one end to the other. Try it with a friend!

MEMORIAL HALL

Admission fee: free. Guided tours that start at the Philadelphia Museum of Art are also available; call 215–684–7500 for more information. Tel. 215–685–0000 (general number).

FRANKFORD ARSENAL,
Bridge and Tacony Streets, Philadelphia

The Frankford Arsenal was located along the Delaware River and Frankford Creek, far enough from the populated area of Philadelphia to allow for future expansion. The Department of Ordnance selected the original twenty-acre site in 1816. The initial buildings of the arsenal consisted of a wharf, officers' quarters, a commandant's house and a powder magazine, all clustered around a large parade ground. The arsenal site continued to grow. By 1861, the depot had developed into a manufacturing facility, churning out percussion caps, paper fuses and other munitions. The arsenal's staff also tested weapons and stored munitions for distribution to army posts. Captain Josiah Gorgas, a Pennsylvania native, was in command of the arsenal in 1861, but resigned on April 3. His wife was the daughter of the governor of Alabama, so Gorgas decided to offer his services to the new Southern Confederacy. Gorgas served as the Confederacy's Chief of Ordnance with the final rank of brigadier general.

Beginning in the early 1960s, the arsenal's functions were gradually transferred to other facilities. When the arsenal closed in 1977, it consisted of 246 buildings located on more than 110 acres. Known today as the Arsenal Business Center, the site and its buildings are being used by private companies. If you wish to tour the site, you must call ahead for permission. The contact person is Mark Hankin, president of the directing company.

Tel. 215–537–8400.

INDEPENDENCE NATIONAL HISTORICAL PARK, 313 Walnut Street, Philadelphia, PA 19106

Although its main focus is on the colonial period of the city's history, the park contains a few sites that have Civil War connections.

Independence Hall, first known as the Pennsylvania State House, was built in the years 1732–1756. Most Americans know that the Declaration of Independence was signed within its walls and that the Continental Congress used the hall as its meeting place. It also served as the first Capitol from 1790 to 1800, before the government moved to Washington, D.C. Most Americans do not know that on February 22, 1861, President-elect Abraham Lincoln, en route to Washington and his March 4 inaugural, stopped in Philadelphia. A platform was erected in front of the hall and Lincoln addressed the assembled crowd, then helped to raise a large American flag specially made for this event. A bronze plaque marking the spot where Lincoln stood is embedded in the sidewalk.

Following Lincoln's assassination, his funeral train came to Philadelphia as part of the dead president's long journey home to Illinois. By the time the train arrived on Saturday, April 22, the city was draped in black mourning crepe. The train from Harrisburg arrived at the Broad and Prime Street Station at 4:30 that afternoon. From the depot, the funeral procession, totaling some thirty carriages and 25,000 soldiers, marched through the crowded streets to Independence Hall; even rooftops were burgeoning with some of the estimated half million onlookers. The hearse finally reached the hall at 8:30. Here, members of the Union League carried the casket into the elaborately decorated central hall, which included the Liberty Bell. Ticket holders were permitted to view the martyred president until ten that night. The hall opened at six on Sunday morning; by 11 A.M., the double lines of people wishing to see the president extended to both the Schuylkill and Delaware Rivers. The casket remained open to viewing until 2 A.M. Monday, by which time some 144,000 people were estimated to have filed by. The president's casket then was moved to the Kensington depot and placed aboard the funeral train, which departed for Trenton, New Jersey.

Independence Hall was the focal point of another celebration a year after the end of the Civil War. Pennsylvania was one of only two Northern states to issue battleflags to the regiments throughout the war. By mid-1865, the state-issued flags had been turned over to the state military department as each unit mustered out of service and returned home. The state government decided to have a military parade in Philadelphia on July 4, 1866, to precede a formal ceremony in which the flags would be returned to state care.

Major General Winfield S. Hancock was selected as marshal of the parade, which included Generals George G. Meade, James S. Negley, Robert Patterson, Charles T. Campbell, David M. Gregg, John W. Geary, Samuel W. Crawford and John R. Brooke. Governor Andrew G. Curtin also rode in the parade, which featured hundreds of veterans proudly carrying their battle-scarred flags. Orphans from the state's newly established schools also were featured.

The parade began at 10 A.M. as formations of color bearers emerged from side streets and began moving north on Broad Street through Penn Square (now City Hall). The parade turned east on Arch Street to Twelfth Street, then proceeded south on Twelfth to Chestnut. Here the column turned east on Chestnut to Second Street, then followed Second southward to Walnut, where it turned west to the gateway at Independence Square, an hour after the start.

The veterans moved north along a gravel pathway to the heavily decorated statehouse. A wooden amphitheater seating 6,000 spectators had been erected in front of the building. As the Handel and Haydn Musical Society played for the occasion, the color bearers massed along the walkway, and the crowds cheered lustily as each general officer rode into the area. Following a welcoming speech and a prayer, General Meade took a flag and gave it to Governor Curtin, following his symbolic gesture with an eloquent speech extolling the virtues of Pennsylvania and its role in the preservation of the Union. Governor Curtin replied with an equally patriotic oration. Then followed more music, a prayer, some more music and the benediction. The city newspapers all reported favorably on the festivities, marred only by thunderstorms that prevented an evening fire-works display.

The Liberty Bell sits in a specially designed pavilion across the street from Independence Hall. This bronze bell was commissioned in 1751, but cracked during its test ring. It was recast and hung in the hall's tower in 1753. The bell cracked a second time in 1835; by 1846, the bell was out of use and kept as a national symbol of independence. During the decades before the Civil War, abolitionists began to use the bell as a symbol of their cause; they dubbed it the Liberty Bell, a phrase that has remained to this day.

Tel. 215–597–8974. Web site: www.nps.gov/inde.

MUSICAL FUND SOCIETY HALL, 808 Locust Street, Philadelphia

Built in 1824, this hall is the oldest standing music hall in the United States. The architect William Strickland designed this two-story building with a flat roof, large arched entrance and Corinthian pilasters on the upper reaches. The hall was enlarged in 1847 with a new front and the stage moved to the rear of the building. In June 1856, the newly formed Republican Party held its first national convention in the hall. After some debate, the Republicans nominated John C. Fremont, the famed explorer and army officer, as their first presidential candidate. In 1924, the hall was acquired by the Philadelphia Labor Institute. The building was converted to a warehouse in 1946. It was vacated in 1964 and became a national historic landmark in 1974. The building is now a condominium complex, with only the original facade remaining.

The building is privately owned and not open to public.

MUSICAL FUND SOCIETY HALL

OLD PINE STREET PRESBYTERIAN CHURCH, 412 Pine Street, Philadelphia

Founded on its present site by the Presbyterian Church in 1768, this church was built in 1837 and is of Greek revival design. In the upper vestibule of the church is a plaque containing the names of eighteen men who died during the Civil War; 138 congregation members served in the war.

Hours: Call ahead for details on visiting. Tel. 215–925–8051.

PORTICO ROW, 900–930 Spruce Street, Philadelphia

The houses in this block are Philadelphia's last surviving upscale residential development of the Jacksonian era of the 1830s.

OLD PINE STREET CHURCH

Owner John Savage hired the young architect Thomas U. Walter to design sixteen houses for sale to upper-middle-class professionals. Each pair of adjacent houses has a shared Ionic-style porch. All had brick facades, marble lintels, while each pair of adjacent houses shared a projecting portico (porch) decorated with marble Ionic columns. Inside, the houses were furnished with marble fireplaces and walnut and mahogany doors and trim. Sarah Josepha Hale (1788–1879), editor of the influential *Godey's Lady's Book* from 1828 to 1877, lived at no. 922 from 1858 to 1861. She also crusaded to make Thanksgiving a national holiday.

PORTICO ROW

WALNUT STREET THEATER,
825 Walnut Street, Philadelphia

The oldest playhouse in America in continuous use, this theater opened in 1809. Many of the greatest American thespians played on stage here—Edwin Forrest and Charlotte Cushman among others. During the Civil War, Mrs. Mary Ann Garrettson was manager of the theater. In 1865, she was ousted by the new owners, John S. Clarke and Edwin Booth; the latter was the older brother of John Wilkes Booth.

Hours: The building still houses an active theater, so call ahead for show times and other details of operation and admission prices. Tel. 215–574–3550.

VANISHED CIVIL WAR SITES

BALDWIN LOCOMOTIVE WORKS

Located on the southwest side of Broad Street at its intersection with Spring Garden, the Baldwin Locomotive Works, which began operations in 1832, produced most of the "iron horses" that pulled trains during the Civil War era. In 1928, when the company moved out of the city to Eddystone, there were many brick buildings on the company's twenty acres. The entire site was razed in 1937 to make room for modern construction. A state office building now occupies the core of the old plant site. A bronze statue of Matthias Baldwin that stood in the area was removed to City Hall, where it can be seen today.

To get there, go north on Broad Street from City Hall. At the corner of the Spring Garden Street intersection, the Baldwin plant was located west of Broad Street.

CAMP DISCHARGE

On October 14, 1864, the War Department issued an order that established a post near Philadelphia that would accommodate troops sent to Pennsylvania for discharge or reorganization. The bulk of soldiers affected included those serving on detached duty when their units were mustered out of service, sick or wounded soldiers in hospitals when their units went home, and returned prisoners from Andersonville and other camps in the South. The post thus established would house these soldiers until their discharge records were compiled and they were well enough to travel.

The site chosen for this camp was located on the top of a bluff overlooking the Schuylkill River, on land owned by local farmers, William Hanna and Joseph Kirkner. The ground was leveled and laborers erected wooden barracks on three sides of a parade ground that faced the river. Lieutenant Colonel John Hancock, a brother of Major General Winfield S. Hancock, was placed in command of the post, which opened in November 1864. Originally christened Camp Spring Mill, the camp was later called Camp Discharge. It remained active until closed in July 1865. Some of the barracks were bought and transferred to Conshohocken, where they became living quarters for mill workers.

Today, the site is incorporated in the golf course area of the Philadelphia Country Club, a private organization. The Country Club, aware of the historical use of the site, is searching for more information so that tablets can be erected to mark the camp's location.

CONTINENTAL HOTEL

Located at the corner of Ninth and Chestnut Streets, this new hotel was finished in 1860. It had 476 guest rooms that could accommodate 700 people. When President-elect Lincoln stopped in Philadelphia en route to Washington, he stayed at the Continental on February 21, 1861. Lincoln made a public address from the hotel's balcony to a large crowd assembled to wish him well; a plaque commemorates the speech. In March 1864, Confederate Colonel Basil W. Duke, captured in John Hunt Morgan's raid in June 1863, stayed at the Continental on March 3, 1864, and was cheered by "disloyal citizens." Later that same month, on March 22, Lieutenant General Ulysses S. Grant and staff lodged at the hotel en route for Washington.

The modern Ben Franklin Hotel–Apartment complex currently occupies the site of the Continental.

JAY COOKE & COMPANY

At 118 South Third Street, adjoining Girard Bank, was the Civil War–period office of Jay Cooke & Company, a banking concern founded in 1861 by Cooke (1821–1905), an Ohio-born financier. Noting that the government was having difficulty raising money to finance the war effort, Cooke approached Secretary of the Treasury Salmon P. Chase and offered his help. Cooke began a fund-raising drive to help finance the war through the sale of government bonds, for which his company became the sole agent. Cooke's national advertising campaign was hugely successful, garnering an estimated $1.5 billion for the war effort. After expenses, Cooke's firm made a profit of only $220,000, about one-sixteenth of one percent of all sales.

The site is now a part of the green expanse of Independence National Historical Park.

COOPER SHOP VOLUNTEER REFRESHMENT SALOON

The Cooper Shop Volunteer Refreshment Saloon opened on May 26, 1861, in a building used as a cooperage by Cooper & Pearce. Its location was on Otsego Street, some 50 yards south of Washington Avenue. The saloon dispensed food to passing soldiers, both individuals and entire regiments. It is estimated that the Cooper Shop provided 400,000 meals. The saloon was in an excellent location on Washington Avenue, at the foot of which ferryboats landed troops heading for Washington. From here, the men would be loaded onto cars of the Philadelphia, Wilmington and Baltimore Railroad.

The construction of I–95 covered the site once occupied by the Cooper Shop.

WILLIAM CRAMP & SONS SHIP AND ENGINE BUILDING COMPANY

Together with the United States Navy Yard, the William Cramp plant, located on the Delaware River at the foot of Norris Street, built and refitted warships during the Civil War. Among the important vessels constructed by Cramp & Sons were the iron-clad *New Ironsides*, sloop *Chattanooga* and gunboat *Wyalusing*. The Cramp establishment was at this site from 1830 until 1927, when a sharp drop in steel construction owing to the Washington Naval Treaty forced the plant to close.

The Cramp establishment was located in the section of the city now known as Fishtown. I–95 runs through the site, but several buildings remain. Traces of the old shipways are still visible as well. The site is adjacent to Penn Treaty Park.

FREE MILITARY SCHOOL

Formed under the aegis of the Philadelphia Supervisory Committee for Recruiting Colored Regiments, this school was designed to assist white soldiers who wished to obtain officers' commissions in the new black regiments being formed in the North. Major George L. Stearns, chief recruiting officer for the commonwealth's black troops, was placed in charge of the school,

SITE OF WILLIAM CRAMP & SONS SHIP AND ENGINE BUILDING COMPANY

which was located at 1210 Chestnut Street. During its two-week course, applicants intensively studied tactics and military protocol. When finished, they were sent to Washington to appear before an examining board, which tested each applicant; if passed, the soldier was commissioned according to his individual achievement in the exam. The Philadelphia school also recommended its "graduates." The school opened on December 29, 1863, and was closed on the last day of December 1864.

The site of the school is now a commercial enterprise.

HORSTMANN BROTHERS & COMPANY

Located at Fifth and Cherry Streets, this military goods company had been founded in 1816 by William H. Horstmann, a German immigrant. He was a passementier by trade and the original business concentrated on coach lace and fancy woven military goods. Horstmann was originally located on North Third Street,

1860s VIEW OF HORSTMANN FACTORY

then on Germantown Road. Horstmann retired from work in 1850; his sons, Sigmund and William J., continued the business, expanding into a full line of military goods, including insignia, swords, drums, flags and uniforms. They erected a modern factory in 1857 at Fifth and Cherry Streets, which shifted into high gear during the war years. A branch in New York City added to the firm's wealth. During the Civil War, Horstmann received large contracts for federal government flags, and also made them for Pennsylvania and New Jersey.

The Horstmann firm survived until 1947, when it declared bankruptcy and its remaining assets were sold at public auction.

The Horstmann factory at Fifth and Cherry Streets was located on part of the site of the United States Mint's present building.

THE LINCOLN INSTITUTE

Located at 308 South Eleventh Street, this school was designed for orphans of slain Civil War veterans. In addition to providing education, the institute would also serve as the temporary home for those who became apprenticed to local tradesmen. The cost per pupil was $3 per week, which included board, bedding and washing. The students went to class five evenings a week and worked during the day.

MERCHANTS' HOTEL

William Strickland designed this large five-story hotel with a colonnade at ground level and a recessed second-story balcony. Built in 1837 at 40–50 North Fourth Street, this hotel was the largest and most prominent hotel in the city. It served as James Buchanan's presidential headquarters during the 1856 election. Sadly, the hotel was destroyed in a 1966 fire.

MOWER U.S. GENERAL HOSPITAL

The single largest army hospital in the Philadelphia area was Mower Hospital, which opened in January 1863 and absorbed patients from several of the city's smaller military hospitals. The twenty-seven-acre site, located in Chestnut Hill, was bounded by Abington and Springfield Avenues, the track of the Reading Railroad (now the SEPTA Wyndmoor Station) and County Line Road (present-day Stenton Avenue). The main hospital complex was built in the shape of a giant rectangle. In the middle were the administration buildings, while each of the forty-seven wards extended outward like spokes of a wheel. The wards had room for 4,000 beds. Recently, a Pennsylvania Historical and Museum Commission Historical Marker was erected to indicate the site.

SCHUYLKILL ARSENAL

The Arsenal on the Schuylkill, commonly known as the Schuylkill Arsenal, was founded by the federal government in 1799 when it purchased an eight-acre tract along the Schuylkill River for an arsenal site. Completed in 1806 with four buildings, the original arsenal eventually expanded to twenty-three buildings. After 1816, the arsenal was used exclusively to manufacture and store clothing, blankets, bedding and tents for the army. The arsenal closed and all buildings were demolished in 1962. Its former address was 2620 Gray's Ferry Avenue, at the northwest corner of Peltz Street at Washington Avenue.

Much of the site is now occupied by the Peco Power Generating Plant.

SOLDIERS' HOME

Originally located at Race and Crown, the Soldiers' Home was opened in 1863 to provide a home for disabled soldiers who had received honorable discharges. The facility rapidly outgrew its first location, so in early 1866 the commonwealth gave the organization the old state armory located at Sixteenth and Filbert Streets. During the war, the Filbert Street General Hospital occupied the armory building. The facility remained open until sometime in the 1880s.

The building was torn down to make way for the Pennsylvania Railroad Station, which in turn disappeared when John F. Kennedy Boulevard was created.

UNION VOLUNTEER REFRESHMENT SALOON

The Union Volunteer Refreshment Saloon (VRS) opened on May 21, 1861, and was located in a leased small-boat shop on Swanson Street at Washington Avenue. Barzilai S. Brown, a grocer, developed the idea to systematize the nourishment of passing soldiers after he noticed that many neighborhood families were already doing so. As funds permitted, adjacent buildings were pressed into service as additional space was needed; one was refurbished as a small hospital. The Union VRS dispensed some 900,000 meals and spent more than $100,000 during the course of the war.

Today, the site of the Union VRS has been obliterated by the construction of I–95.

UNITED STATES NAVAL HOME

Located at the southwest corner of Gray's Ferry Avenue and Twenty-fourth Street at Bainbridge Street, the Naval Home was a facility for old, disabled, and retired officers of the U.S. Navy and Marine Corps. The home, originally called the United States Naval Asylum, opened in 1831. Biddle Hall, built in the years 1827–1833, was home to the Naval Academy (1840–1845), then used as a hospital until 1868. William Strickland's design was for the largest Greek revival hospital building in America at the time. It was three stories high and 380 feet wide across the front. The Governor's Residence was added in 1844, as was the Surgeon's Residence. The three main buildings had been surrounded by a twenty-five-acre park, which was enclosed by an iron fence. When the facility shut down in 1976, it was the only retirement home for naval personnel in the country. In 1866, the home contained 120 pensioners.

The buildings are empty and decaying. After the facility closed, a local firm purchased the site and planned to convert the existing buildings into a condominium project while maintaining their historical integrity. Sadly, the project never developed and it appears that the site is a victim of demolition by neglect.

UNITED STATES NAVAL SHIPYARD

The entrance to the United States Naval Shipyard during the Civil War was located at the foot of Federal Street. Here, the main gate pierced a high brick wall that enclosed the eighteen-acre site, which was bounded by Front, Prime and Wharton Streets. Two great ship houses dominated the site, which also included machine shops, barracks and other buildings. During the war, almost 3,000 men were employed. The yard launched eleven warships, including six sloops, two steamers, one steam frigate, one gunboat and the double-turret monitor *Tonawanda*. The yard mechanics also refitted many other vessels during the war. In June 1862, the Philadelphia City Council voted to search for a new site for the naval yard. The selected site at League Island was presented to the Navy Department for approval. The old yard was closed in 1875 when the new location began operating. The land was sold at auction later that year; John C. Bullett, representing the Pennsylvania Railroad Company, paid $1 million for the site. The site of the Navy Yard gradually became landlocked as waterfront reclamation projects pushed dry land eastward.

Today, Pier 55 South Delaware Wharves is located on the modern riverfront equivalent of the yard site.

CEMETERIES

CATHEDRAL CEMETERY, Forty-eighth Street and Lancaster Avenue, Philadelphia, PA 19131

One brevet brigadier general is buried here. St. Clair A. Mulholland (1839–1910) was colonel of the 116th Pennsylvania. He was brevetted brigadier general in March 1865 for gallant meritorious services, and brevetted major general for his services at the Boydton Plank Road (October 27, 1864). He also received a Congressional Medal of Honor for gallantry at Chancellorsville. Buried on South Border, Lot 154.

Hours: Daily during daylight hours. Call ahead for information on visiting. Tel. 215–477–8918.

Directions: Cathedral Cemetery is in West Philadelphia. From the Schuylkill Expressway, exit at Girard Avenue (Route 30). Go west on Gerard to its T-intersection with Lancaster Avenue: The cemetery entrance is immediately ahead of you.

CATHEDRAL CEMETERY

CHRIST CHURCH BURIAL GROUND,
20 North American Street, Philadelphia, PA 19106

This small cemetery contains the graves of two Philadelphia-born Union generals:

Major General George Cadwalader (1806–1879), a city native, was a lawyer and Mexican War veteran before returning to duty in 1861. After brief active field service in 1861, he served on various boards until appointed to the command of troops in Philadelphia in August 1863, a post he held until the end of the war.

Brigadier General George A. McCall (1802–1868) was the first commander of the famous Pennsylvania Reserves in the years 1861–1862. He was captured during the fierce fighting at Glendale on June 30, 1862, and incarcerated until exchanged in August. He returned home and was on sick leave until he resigned in March 1863.

CHRIST CHURCH BURIAL GROUND

Other notables interred here include Benjamin Franklin and his wife, Deborah. The cemetery was established in 1719 on the outskirts of the growing city. Christ Church itself is located at 20 North American Street.

Hours: Call Christ Church for information and accessibility. Tel. 215–922–1695.

Directions: The church itself is on North American Street just off Second Street. The churchyard is located adjacent to Independence Mall, across Arch Street from the U.S. Mint.

CHURCH OF ST. JAMES THE LESS (Episcopal), 3200 West Clearfield Street, Philadelphia

Built in the years 1846–1849, this venerable church is a close copy of a thirteenth-century English parish church, based on plans provided by the Cambridge Camden Society. The American architect added a bay to the nave. Among the burials in the churchyard are the following:

Brigadier General James B. Fry (1827–1894), an Illinois native, graduated from West Point in 1847. During the Civil War, Fry served as chief of staff to Generals Irvin McDowell and Don Carlos Buell. When the Bureau of the Provost Marshal General was created in 1863, Fry was named to command and acted as such until the bureau was discontinued in 1865. He retired in 1881 as colonel in the adjutant general's department. His postwar writings include *McDowell and Tyler in the Campaign of Bull Run* (1884) and *Operations of the Army Under Buell* (1884).

Major General John G. Parke (1827–1900) was born in Coatesville, graduated from West Point in 1849 and served in the Topographical Engineers until 1861. He was promoted to brigadier general of volunteers and served in the Ninth Corps throughout the war, ultimately promoted to major general and in command of the corps. Parke continued in the engineers after the war and retired in 1889. During the last three years of his army career, Parke was superintendent of West Point.

Brevet Brigadier General Benjamin C. Tilghman (1821–1901) was colonel of the 26th Pennsylvania Infantry, then became colonel of the 3rd United States Colored Troops.

Hours: Call ahead for information on visiting the grave sites and church. Tel. 215–229–5767.

Directions: This church is not far from Laurel Hill Cemetery. From Ridge Avenue, branch off on Route 13 (Hunting Park

Avenue), then turn left on West Clearfield. Church of St. James the Less is at the intersection with Thirty-second Street (one block).

FOREST HILLS CEMETERY,
101 Byberry Road, Philadelphia, PA 19116

This cemetery was opened in 1899. Burials include one brevet brigadier general: Samuel K. Schwenk (1842–1915) was lieutenant colonel of the 50th Pennsylvania, and he was promoted to brevet brigadier general in July 1865 for meritorious services during the war. Buried in Wissahickon Section, Lot 396.

Tel. 215–673–5800.

Directions: This cemetery is located just out of the city limits in northeast Philadelphia. From Roosevelt Boulevard (Route 1), exit at Woodhaven Road. Go west a short distance: Woodhaven will turn sharply to the left to become Evans Street, which dead-ends at Byberry Road very quickly. Turn right on Byberry and follow it west to the cemetery.

IVY HILL CEMETERY, 1201 Easton Road,
P.O. Box 27307, Philadelphia, PA 19150

Organized in 1866, this cemetery originally was named the Germantown and Chestnut Hill Cemetery but changed its name in 1871. Burials include the following:

Peter Lyle (1821–1879) was colonel of the 90th Pennsylvania and brevetted a brigadier general in March 1865 for faithful and gallant services in battle. Buried in Section K, Lot 716.

Louis Wagner (1838–1914) was colonel of the 88th Pennsylvania. He was badly wounded at Second Manassas and was unfit for active duty. In 1863, he was named the commander of Camp William Penn, the training camp for the commonwealth's eleven United States Colored Troops regiments. Wagner was brevetted a brigadier general in March 1865. Buried in Section J, Lot 487.

Tel. 215–248–4533.

Directions: From Broad Street, go north on Broad to Cheltenham Avenue (Route 309). Turn left (northwest) on Cheltenham and stay on Cheltenham after Route 309 diverges onto Ogontz. At the intersection with Easton Road, turn left and proceed to the cemetery entrance on the right as you see the cemetery. From the Pennsylvania Turnpike, exit at Fort Washington Interchange (Exit 26) and proceed south on Fort Washington Expressway. Exit south on Easton Road to cemetery.

LAUREL HILL CEMETERY,
3822 Ridge Avenue, Philadelphia, PA 19132

Opened in 1836, Laurel Hill Cemetery was designed by the noted architect John Notman on a rolling bluff overlooking the Schuylkill River. His design was based on London's Kensal Green Cemetery. He wanted enough green space so that each family could have its own plot, surrounded by an iron fence. In Victorian times, thousands visited the cemetery because it meant a quiet stroll in elegant surroundings, which included roads and paths originating from a central circular avenue as well as gazebos and lookout points, exotic trees and shrubs. The cemetery has numerous Civil War dead within its confines. The more important personages herein include the following:

Brevet Brigadier General Henry H. Bingham (1841–1912) was a Philadelphia native educated at Jefferson College (now Washington & Jefferson) in Washington, PA. He was a captain in the 140th Pennsylvania Infantry, then was detached and served on the staff of Major General Winfield S. Hancock as

LAUREL HILL CEMETERY

Judge Advocate. Bingham was brevetted a brigadier general in 1865 for gallant and meritorious services, and awarded a Congressional Medal of Honor for heroic action during the Battle of the Wilderness. After the war, he served in the U.S. House of Representatives from 1879 to 1912. Buried in Section Y, Lot 105.

George A. H. Blake (1810–1884) was colonel of the 1st United States Cavalry and also served on the staff of Major General Alfred Pleasonton. He received two brevets in March 1865: brigadier general for services during the Gettysburg campaign, and major general for meritorious services during the war. Buried in Section H, Lot 68.

Brigadier General Henry Bohlen (1810–1862) was a German immigrant who was elected colonel of the largely German 75th Pennsylvania. His men saw service in the Shenandoah Valley. Promoted to general in April 1862, Bohlen received command of a brigade in the Army of Virginia. During fighting at Freeman's Ford on the Rappahannock River on August 22, 1862, Bohlen was killed as his outnumbered brigade was pushed back across the river. Buried in Section Y, Lot 34.

Gideon Clark (1822–1897) was lieutenant colonel of the 119th Pennsylvania. He was brevetted brigadier general in March 1865 for gallant and meritorious services. Buried in Section 8, Lot 51.

Thomas J. Cram (1804–1883) was a Regular Army engineer and staff officer. He received a brevet brigadier generalship in the volunteer army in March 1865 for faithful and meritorious services, and in 1866 received brevets to brigadier general and major general in the Regular Army. Buried in Section 3, Lot 106.

Major General Samuel W. Crawford (1829–1892), a Franklin County, Pennsylvania, native, graduated from the medical school of the University of Pennsylvania in 1846. He then received an appointment as an army surgeon and was in the garrison of Fort Sumter when the Confederates opened fire on April 12, 1861. In April 1862, Crawford was promoted from major to a brigadier general of volunteers and commanded a brigade in the Army of Virginia, where his men suffered heavy casualties at Cedar Mountain. He led a division of the Twelfth Corps at Antietam then transferred to command of the Pennsylvania Reserves, which he led at Gettysburg. During the remainder of the war, Crawford had command of a division in the Army of the Potomac's Fifth Corps. He remained in the army until retired in 1875. Postwar writings included a memoir of Fort Sumter and a history of the Chancellorsville and Gettysburg campaigns. Buried in Section L, Lot 69.

Alexander Cummings (1810–1879) was colonel of the 19th Pennsylvania Cavalry then served as Superintendent of Colored

Troops for the Department of Arkansas. He received a brevet brigadier generalship in April 1865 for meritorious services. Buried in Section I, Lot 224.

Rear Admiral John A. B. Dahlgren (1809–1870) was the son of the Swedish counsel to the United States and was born in Philadelphia. He loved the sea and entered American naval service in 1826. He rose through the ranks and became an ordnance expert, inventing bronze boat howitzers and rifles, iron smooth-bore shellguns and iron rifles, all popularly known as *Dahlgren guns*. In 1861, Dahlgren was placed in command of the Washington Navy Yard; on July 16, 1862, he became chief of the Bureau of Ordnance. In February 1863, he was promoted to rear admiral and took command of the South Atlantic Blockading Squadron. After the war, he remained on active duty and died of heart disease in 1870. Buried in Section L, Lots 50–54.

Benezet F. Foust (1840–1870) was major of the 88th Pennsylvania, then served in the Veteran Reserve Corps as a lieutenant colonel. He was brevetted brigadier general in March 1865 for gallant and meritorious services in a number of engagements, including Gettysburg. Buried in Section Y, Lot 84.

Brevet Brigadier General Louis R. Francine (1837–1863) was a civil engineer from Philadelphia who became colonel of the 7th New Jersey Infantry. He was mortally wounded at Gettysburg on July 2, 1863, and died two weeks later. Buried in Section Y, Lot 144.

Brevet Brigadier General Edgar M. Gregory (1804–1871) was colonel of the 91st Pennsylvania Infantry. He was brevetted brigadier general for service at the Battle of Poplar Spring Church, then brevetted major general for his work at the Battle of Five Forks. Buried in Section 16, Lot 313.

Caldwell K. Hall (1839–1870), lieutenant colonel of the 14th New Jersey, was brevetted brigadier general for gallant services at the Battle of Monocacy, Maryland. Buried in Section G, Lot 245.

Brevet Brigadier General John William Hofmann (1824–1902) was colonel of the 56th Pennsylvania. His regiment fired the first infantry shots of the Battle of Gettysburg. After the war, he was a hosiery merchant and wrote numerous articles about Gettysburg, defending the action of his regiment against claims from Iron Brigade veterans that their units fired the first shots of the infantry battle at Gettysburg. Buried in Section G, Lot 63.

Brigadier General Thomas L. Kane (1822–1883) was an avowed abolitionist whose father, a federal judge in eastern Pennsylvania, jailed his son for failing to uphold the Fugitive Slave Law. Kane drifted west and linked up with the Mormons; he was instrumental in finding a compromise that avoided bloodshed when U.S. Army forces were sent to Utah in 1858. He assisted in recruiting the famed Pennsylvania Bucktails (13th Pennsylvania Reserves) and became lieutenant colonel of the regiment. He was wounded and captured near Harrisonburg, Virginia, in June 1862. Following his exchange, Kane was promoted to brigadier general and commanded a Twelfth Corps brigade at Chancellorsville and Gettysburg. Health reasons compelled his resignation in November 1863. He was at first buried in his brother's tomb at Laurel Hill, but later reinterred to a chapel in Kane, Pennsylvania, a small village he had founded before the war.

Oliver B. Knowles (1842–1866) was colonel of the 21st Pennsylvania Cavalry and was brevetted brigadier general in March 1865 for gallant and meritorious services. Buried in Section K, Lot 106.

William D. Lewis, Jr. (1827–1872) was colonel of the 110th Pennsylvania and was brevetted brigadier general in March 1865 for gallant and meritorious services. Buried in Section A, Lots 91–102.

RESTING PLACE OF COL. OLIVER KNOWLES

Major General George G. Meade (1815–1872) was born in Cadiz, Spain, the son of a Philadelphia merchant. Meade graduated from West Point in 1835 and left the army a year later to pursue a civil engineering career. He reentered military service during the Mexican War, then served as an engineer on the Atlantic Coast and Great Lakes. Appointed a brigadier general in 1861, Meade led a brigade of the Pennsylvania Reserves; he was wounded at Glendale on June 30, 1862. After service at Second Manassas, Meade led the division at South Mountain, Antietam and Fredericksburg. He was promoted to major general in the fall

RESTING PLACE OF MAJ. GENERAL GEORGE G. MEADE

1862 and in early 1863 given command of the Fifth Corps, which he led at Chancellorsville. On June 28, 1863, Meade was unexpectedly placed in command of the Army of the Potomac, which he led for the rest of the war. His victory at Gettysburg repelled Lee's invasion of Pennsylvania, but a slow pursuit and backbiting by subordinates through the winter impaired his reputation. Overshadowed by Grant, Meade's handling of the army during the 1864–65 campaign has been largely overlooked by many historians. After the war, Meade commanded various military departments. He died of pneumonia while in command of the Division of the Atlantic, headquartered in Philadelphia. Buried in Section L, Lots 1–7.

Brigadier General James St. Clair Morton (1829–1864) entered the University of Pennsylvania at age fourteen, then went to West Point, graduating second in the class of 1851. After a number of engineering assignments, Morton entered active military service in June 1862 as chief engineer of the Army of the Ohio, then in the same capacity in the Army of the Cumberland. He had been promoted to brigadier general of volunteers in April 1863, but declined the appointment and reverted to his Regular Army rank of major. In January 1864, Morton was transferred to Washington, D.C., as assistant to the department's chief engineer. In May, he was assigned to the Ninth Corps as chief engineer. He was killed on June 17 in front of Petersburg as he reconnoitered the terrain prior to an attack. Buried in Section G, Lot 179.

Brigadier General Henry M. Naglee (1815–1886), an 1835 West Point graduate, was a civil engineer until the Mexican War, when he led a volunteer company. He settled in California thereafter, becoming a brigadier general of volunteers in early 1862. His Fourth Corps brigade suffered heavy casualties at Fair Oaks (May 31, 1862). Thereafter, his active military service centered on coastal Virginia and North Carolina until September 1863, when he was relieved as a result of a political disagreement with Virginia Governor Francis H. Pierpont. Naglee went back to California, working in banking and grape growing until his death. Buried in Section 1, Lots 147–50.

Brigadier General Joshua T. Owen (1821–1887) was a Welsh immigrant who came to America in 1830. He taught at Chestnut Hill Academy and was a member of the Pennsylvania legislature from 1857 to 1859. He was colonel of the 24th Pennsylvania, then of the largely Irish 69th Pennsylvania. He served with the Army of the Potomac and was promoted to brigade command in November 1862. He was relieved of command a few days before Gettysburg, and brought up before a court martial for disobedience of orders at Cold Harbor, Virginia, in June

1864. The court failed to reach a verdict before Owen was honorably mustered out of service in July. He resumed a law practice and in 1871 founded the New York *Daily Register*, which became the official publication of the New York courts in 1873. Buried in Section 5, Lot 81.

William Painter (1838–1884) served on the staffs of Generals Edward O. C. Ord and James B. Ricketts, in addition to serving in the quartermaster's department. He was brevetted brigadier general in March 1865 for faithful and meritorious services during the war. Buried in Section T, Lot 125.

Brigadier General Francis E. Patterson (1821–1862), a son of General Robert Patterson, was also a brother-in-law of General John J. Abercrombie. Patterson served in the Regular Army until 1857, when he resigned to return to civilian life. In 1861, he became colonel of the 17th Pennsylvania, then was promoted to brigadier general in April 1862. He led a brigade in the Army of the Potomac's Third Corps, fighting at Williamsburg and Fair Oaks. On November 22, 1862, the general was found dead in his tent, slain by the accidental discharge of his pistol. Buried in Section K, Lots 38–51.

Major General Robert Patterson (1792–1881) was born in Ireland; his family fled to America after the failed 1798 rebellion. Patterson served in the War of 1812 and commanded a division in the Mexican War. In 1861, he was the oldest major general in service and was placed in command of the forces operating in the Shenandoah Valley. His failure to prevent Joseph Johnston's Confederates from moving to Manassas was widely criticized and his commission was allowed to expire soon thereafter. Patterson returned to civilian life and became a prosperous mill operator. Buried in Section K, Lot 38.

Robert E. Patterson (1830–1906), a son of Major General Robert Patterson, was colonel of the 115th Pennsylvania. He was brevetted brigadier general in March 1865 for meritorious services. Buried in Section K, Lot 38.

Lieutenant General John C. Pemberton (1814–1881) was a Philadelphia native who graduated from West Point and fought in the Mexican War. He had married a Virginia woman in 1848; this union probably influenced his resignation from the U.S. Army in 1861. He joined the Confederacy and was rapidly promoted to lieutenant general. As commander of the Department of Mississippi and East Louisiana, Pemberton led the defenses of Vicksburg against Ulysses S. Grant. He surrendered the garrison on July 4, 1863. This was his last active command and he resigned his general's commission in 1864. After the war, he lived in Virginia at first, then returned to the Keystone State. Buried in Section 9, Lot 53.

Charles M. Prevost (1818–1887) was colonel of the 118th Pennsylvania and, after a wound prevented further active service, served as colonel of the 16th Veteran Reserve Corps. He was brevetted brigadier general in March 1865 for meritorious services. Buried in Section B, Lot 64.

William R. Price (1836–1881) started his military career in the 3rd Pennsylvania Cavalry, then served on General William W. Averell's staff, and finally at the Cavalry Bureau in Washington. He was brevetted brigadier general in March 1865 for faithful and meritorious services. Buried in Section I, Lot 5.

Joseph Roberts (1814–1898), an 1835 West Point graduate, was colonel of the 3rd Pennsylvania Heavy Artillery and also was commandant of Fort Monroe. He was brevetted brigadier general in the Regular Army in March 1865 and in the volunteers a month later. Buried in Section 3, Lot 41.

Major General Charles F. Smith (1807–1862) was an 1825 graduate of West Point. He served gallantly in the Mexican War and in 1861 became a brigadier general of volunteers. He served under former pupils Ulysses S. Grant and William T. Sherman at Forts Henry and Donelson. Smith suffered a minor skin scrape that became infected and caused his death in April 1862. Buried in Section X, Lots 438–40.

Brigadier General Alfred Sully (1820–1879) graduated from West Point in 1841 and fought in the Mexican War. In 1861, he became colonel of the 1st Minnesota and was soon promoted to brigade command in the Second Corps, seeing action on the Peninsula, Antietam, Fredericksburg and Chancellorsville. He was then transferred to the Department of Dakota as commander of the department, and led successful expeditions against the Sioux. He served continuously in western commands, and was in charge of Fort Vancouver, Washington, when he died in 1879. Buried in Section A, Lot 41.

Robert Thompson (1828–1881), lieutenant colonel of the 115th Pennsylvania, was brevetted brigadier general in March 1865 for meritorious services. Buried in Section G, Lot 267.

George A. Townsend (1841–1914) was a young war correspondent who wrote for several newspapers during the war, using the pen name Gath. In 1884, Townsend purchased land on South Mountain, Maryland, near the site of the fighting at Crampton's Gap. In addition to a home, Townsend constructed a memorial to 157 war correspondents, both Union and Confederate. This monument and land was eventually deeded to the federal government and is now operated by the National Park Service. Buried in Section 9, Lot 98.

Brigadier General Hector Tyndale (1821–1880), the son of Irish immigrants, had become a well-known exporter of glass and ceramics by 1861, when he got caught up in the war fever and joined the 28th Pennsylvania. For gallantry in action, especially at Antietam, where he was wounded and had three horses shot from under him, Tyndale became a brigadier general and led a brigade in the Twelfth Corps. By early 1864, Tyndale was a division commander in Tennessee, but went home on a leave of absence due to illness and never returned to active duty. He again became a prominent Philadelphia merchant after the war. Buried in Section H, Lots 1 and 2.

Langhorne Wister (1834–1891), colonel of the 150th Pennsylvania (Bucktails), was at Gettysburg on the morning of July 1, 1863, when old John Burns decided to take up arms and fight. As the 150th marched by, Burns put on his Sunday best—tails and tall hat—and fell in with Wister's regiment. Colonel Wister asked the old man, "Can you shoot?" Burns proudly responded, "Give me a chance and I'll show you who can shoot." Wister nodded and sent Burns off to join the lines of the Iron Brigade where he proved his boast. Wister himself was brevetted brigadier general in March 1865 for distinguished gallantry at Gettysburg as well as other meritorious service. Buried in Section L, Lots 316–18.

Hours: Tuesday–Saturday, 9:30 A.M. to 1:30 P.M.; closed on Sunday, Monday and holidays. Tel. 215–228–8200.

Directions: Go north on East River Drive to Ferry Road. Turn right on Ferry and go one block to Ridge Avenue. Turn right on Ridge: cemetery entrance is about half a mile on the right.

MEMORIAL CHURCH OF ST. LUKE THE BELOVED PHYSICIAN, 1946 Welsh Road, Philadelphia, PA 19115

Memorial Church was built in 1861; the church graveyard contains the following grave:

Pennock Huey (1828–1903) was colonel of the 8th Pennsylvania Cavalry and was brevetted brigadier general in March 1865 for gallant and meritorious services.

In addition to General Huey's grave, also nearby are the graves of father and son, killed in two separate battles on the same day.

Hours: Call ahead for permission to visit the church graveyard. Tel. 215–969–3645.

MOUNT MORIAH CEMETERY,
6201 Kingsessing Avenue, Philadelphia, PA 19142

Founded in 1854, this burial ground is divided by Cobb's Creek, the line of demarcation between Philadelphia and Delaware counties. Burials in this cemetery include the following brevet brigadier generals:

Edwin R. Biles (1828–1883) was colonel of the 99th Pennsylvania Infantry. He was a Mexican War veteran and was brevetted for gallantry at Deep Bottom, Virginia. After the war, he worked as a clerk in the City of Philadelphia's Recorder's Office. Buried in Section 30, Lot 51.

MOUNT MORIAH CEMETERY

George W. Gile (1830–1896) was colonel of the 88th Pennsylvania Infantry. He was severely wounded at Antietam and transferred to the Veteran Reserve Corps. As colonel of the 9th Regiment, V.R.C., Gile was brevetted for gallantry during the Confederate attack on Washington, D.C., in July 1863. A stage actor prior to 1861, Gile remained in the Regular Army and retired as a colonel in 1870. Buried in Section 203, Lot 37.

John K. Murphy (1796–1876) was young enough to fight in the War of 1812 before joining the Union army in 1861 as colonel of the 29th Pennsylvania Infantry. His civilian career included stints as a police marshal and bathhouse proprietor. Buried in Section 128, Lot 3.

Charles F. Ruff (1818–1885) fought in the Mexican War, then became lieutenant colonel of the 3rd United States Cavalry. During the Civil War he was a mustering and disbursing officer in Philadelphia, and later a provost marshal in western Pennsylvania. Ruff also served on the staff of Major General Darius N. Couch as an assistant inspector general. He retired in 1864. Buried in Section 105, Lot 37.

Robert E. Winslow (1829–1893) was lieutenant colonel of the 68th Pennsylvania Infantry and brevetted a brigadier general for faithful and meritorious service during the war. Buried in Section 116, Lot 227C.

Hours: Office is open Monday–Friday, 9 A.M. to 4 P.M. The cemetery grounds are open during daylight hours seven days a week. Call ahead for staff assistance in locating grave sites. Tel. 215–729–1295.

Directions: Proceed south on Woodland Avenue to Fifty-eighth Street. Turn right on Fifty-eighth and take the first left onto Kingsessing. Cemetery entrance is on your right at Sixty-second Street.

MOUNT PEACE CEMETERY,
3111 West Lehigh Avenue, Philadelphia, PA 19132

This cemetery was organized in 1865. Burials include the following:

John F. Ballier (1815–1893) was colonel of the 98th Pennsylvania. He was brevetted brigadier general on July 13, 1864, for distinguished gallantry during Grant's campaign against Richmond and Petersburg. Buried in Section I, Lot 430.

Turner G. Morehead (1814–1892), colonel of the 106th Pennsylvania, was brevetted brigadier general in March 1865 for faithful and meritorious services. Buried in Section R, Lot 161.

Tel. 215–379–1600.

Directions: Proceed north on Broad Street to Lehigh Avenue. Turn left on Lehigh to cemetery entrance past Thirty-first Street on your right.

MOUNT PEACE CEMETERY

PHILADELPHIA NATIONAL CEMETERY, Haines Street and Limekiln Pike, Philadelphia, PA 19138

This small national cemetery was organized in 1885. Union soldiers who died in military hospitals in the city were first buried in seven different cemeteries: Glenwood, Lafayette, Lebanon, Mount Moriah, Odd Fellows, United American Mechanics Association and Woodland. Three other cemeteries—Bristol, Chester and Whitehall—joined the previous seven. These cemeteries were loosely organized as a national cemetery in 1874. The government acquired the current property in 1885, and most soldiers from the other ten lots were removed to this location by 1892. Burials continued until 1962, when the cemetery was filled.

One brevet brigadier general is buried here. Galusha Pennypacker (1844–1916) entered service in 1861 as the sixteen-year-old quartermaster sergeant of the 9th Pennsylvania. He then recruited a company for the 97th Pennsylvania and was elected captain. He was promoted to major in October 1861 and served with his regiment along the Atlantic seaboard, taking part in siege operations at Charleston. Promoted to colonel by the time the 97th was transferred to the Army of the James, Pennypacker was wounded four times during operations around Petersburg. He was badly wounded during the assault on Fort Fisher, North Carolina, in January 1865; it was feared that he would succumb to his wounds. He was promoted to brigadier general on April 28, a month before his twenty-first birthday. Pennypacker transferred to the Regular Army after the war and served until his retirement in 1883.

Burials in this cemetery also include 224 Confederate soldiers. The United Daughters of the Confederacy erected a monument to their dead, who were moved to this cemetery after dying in the military hospitals throughout the city. The monument lists 187 known names and four unknowns.

The cemetery is managed by Beverly National Cemetery, 916 Bridgeboro Road, Beverly, NJ 08010. Tel. 609–877–5460.

Directions: From Broad Street, proceed north to Stenton Avenue. Turn left (west) on Stenton and proceed to Ogontz Street. Turn right (north) on Ogontz, then left on Haines (five blocks). Cemetery entrance is straight ahead at Haines and Limekiln Pike.

ST. DOMINIC'S CATHOLIC CHURCH,
8504 Frankford Avenue, Philadelphia, PA 19136

Thomas Kilby Smith (1820–1887), born in Massachusetts and raised in Ohio, became colonel of the 54th Ohio in 1861. He served in the Army of the Tennessee and performed steady, capable service. He was promoted to brigadier general in August 1863 and brevetted major general in March 1865. He led his regiment, brigade, and later a small division in the Red River campaign. Smith was consul to Panama after the war, settled in the Torresdale section of Philadelphia, and died in New York City. Buried in Section G, Range 10, center of Lots 16–18.

Hours: Call ahead for permission to visit and hours when a guide can show General Smith's grave. Tel. 215–624–5502.

Directions: From I–95, exit at Academy Road, then left (south) on Frankford Avenue to the church, about five blocks.

ST. LUKE'S EPISCOPAL CHURCHYARD,
5421 Germantown Avenue, Philadelphia, PA 19144

St. Luke's graveyard includes George W. Gowen (1840–1865), colonel of the 48th Pennsylvania. He was killed during the April 2, 1865, assault on Petersburg, and was posthumously given a brevet brigadier generalship.

Hours: Call ahead for information on visiting. Tel. 215–844–8544.

ST. PAUL'S EPISCOPAL CHURCHYARD,
7809 Old York Road, Elkins Park, PA 19027

The graveyard includes Ario Pardee, Jr. (1839–1901), colonel of the 147th Pennsylvania. He was awarded a brevet brigadier generalship on January 12, 1865, for special gallantry during the Battle of Peach Tree Creek (July 20, 1864).

Hours: Call ahead for information on visiting; ask for Harriet Schiffer. Tel. 215–635–4185.

ST. PETER'S EPISCOPAL CHURCHYARD,
313 Pine Street, Philadelphia, PA 19106

This cemetery holds the grave of John Markoe (1840–1893), lieutenant colonel of the 71st Pennsylvania. He was brevetted brigadier general in March 1865 for gallant and meritorious services at the Battle of Fredericksburg.

Hours: Call ahead for information on visiting. Tel. 215–925–5968.

WEST LAUREL HILL CEMETERY,
215 Belmont Avenue, Bala Cynwyd, PA 19004

Burials here include the following:

Herman Haupt (1817–1905) was a brilliant engineer, graduating from West Point at the age of eighteen. A year later, Haupt was already assistant engineer of the Commonwealth of Pennsylvania and published books and articles on bridge construction. Haupt was instrumental in the design and construction of several railroads in New England, New York and Pennsylvania. In 1862, Haupt was asked to be the chief of construction and transporta-

ST. PETER'S EPISCOPAL CHURCHYARD

WEST LAUREL HILL CEMETERY

tion for the United States Military Railroads. Although promoted to brigadier general in September 1862, Haupt never accepted the rank and preferred to serve as a civilian so he could also devote time to his own projects. Still, Haupt's enlightened leadership brought order to military rail lines in Virginia until he returned to civilian life in September 1863. Haupt continued his railroad work, delved into oil pipeline construction, and pioneered the use of compressed air for motors and mine machinery.

William A. Leech (1832–1870), lieutenant colonel of the 90th Pennsylvania, received a brevet brigadier generalship in March 1865 for gallant and meritorious services. Buried in the Merion Section, Lot 95.

James Stewart, Jr. (1840–1930) was colonel of the 9th New Jersey and was brevetted brigadier general in March 1865 for meritorious services. Buried in the Moreland Section, Lot 63.

Hours: Daily during daylight hours, but call ahead for more information. Tel. 610–664–1591.

Directions: From Schuylkill Expressway, exit at Belmont Avenue and proceed up the hill: cemetery entrance is on the left.

WESTMINSTER CEMETERY,
701 Belmont Avenue, Bala Cynwyd, PA 19004

Established in 1894, this suburban cemetery includes one brevet brigadier general. Peter Fritz, Jr. (1838–1907), lieutenant colonel of the 99th Pennsylvania, was brevetted brigadier general in March 1865 for gallantry and good conduct in front of Petersburg, September 10, 1864. Buried in the Lake View Section, Lot 194.

Tel. 610–667–0550.

Directions: From the Valley Forge area, take the Schuylkill Expressway (Route 76) east to Exit 31 (Belmont Avenue). At the base of the exit ramp, turn right on Belmont Avenue. Proceed beneath the overpass and through two traffic lights. The cemetery is a quarter mile on the left. From the south (Philadelphia), use Exit 31 (Belmont Avenue); turn left, beneath the overpass, through two traffic lights. The cemetery is a quarter mile on the left.

WISTAR INSTITUTE,
3601 Spruce Street, Philadelphia, PA 19104

The nation's oldest independent biomedical research institute, the Wistar Institute of Anatomy and Biology's history extends back to the colonial period and Dr. Caspar Wistar. His great-nephew, Isaac Jones Wistar (1827–1905), served in the Civil War, first as a colonel on the 71st Pennsylvania and later as a brigadier general. Wistar led a brigade of the Seventh Corps and later in the Eighteenth Corps until he resigned in September 1864 because of wounds. Successful in business after the war, Wistar endowed the institute and named it after his famous great-uncle. Isaac Wistar's cremated remains are placed there and his military papers are available for research.

Hours: Weekdays 9:00 A.M. to 5:00 P.M. Tel. 215-898-3700, ask for Nina Long.

WOODLANDS CEMETERY,
4000 Woodland Avenue, Philadelphia, PA 19104–4560

The Woodlands Cemetery was incorporated in 1840 and still operates as a nonprofit company. The burial grounds surround the Woodlands Mansion, an elegant structure erected between 1788 and 1813 by William Hamilton. A friend of many prominent Americans of his day, Hamilton was an avid botanist and introduced many rare plants to America. Both the house and remaining stable (ca. 1792) are national historic landmarks.

A number of prominent Americans of the Civil War period are buried in Woodlands. These include the following:

Major General John J. Abercrombie (1798–1877), a Baltimore native, graduated from West Point in 1822 and served in the Regular Army until the Civil War, when he was promoted to

WOODLANDS CEMETERY

brigadier general of volunteers in August 1861. He was a brigade commander in the Fourth Army Corps and fought at Fair Oaks, then was elevated to divisional command. His service was then restricted to the defenses of Washington and other rear areas. Abercrombie was brevetted brigadier general in the Regular Army in 1865 and retired in 1866. Buried in Section H, Lot 311–313.

Brevet Brigadier General Hartman Bache (1798–1872) was an 1818 graduate of West Point. He served in the Corps of Topographical Engineers and retired as colonel in 1867. Bache was a great-grandson of Benjamin Franklin and a brother-in-law of Major General George G. Meade. Buried in Section 1, Lot 831.

Major General David B. Birney (1825–1864), Union division and corps commander in the Army of the Potomac and Army of the James; he died of disease in October 1864. He began the war as colonel of the 23rd Pennsylvania, then was promoted to brigadier and major general, commanding a brigade and division in the Third Corps. His division became part of the Second Corps in 1864; he was later transferred to command of the Tenth Corps, Army of the James, at which post he was serving when he died of malaria. Buried in Section CC, Lot 52.

John H. Brinton (1832–1907), outstanding U.S. army surgeon during the Civil War, founder of the U.S. Army Medical Museum, and major contributor to *The Medical and Surgical History of the War of the Rebellion*. Buried in Section N, Lot 239–242.

Brevet Major General George H. Crosman (1799–1882) was an 1823 graduate of West Point. During the war, he was the Chief Quartermaster of the Philadelphia Depot, better known as the Schuylkill Arsenal. Buried in Section F, Lot 627.

Jacob M. DaCosta (1833–1900), surgeon and medical author who noted the Civil War "irritable heart of the soldier" (Post-Traumatic Stress Disorder). Buried in Section G, Lot 368–371.

Brevet Brigadier General John Ely (1816–1869) was colonel of the 23rd Pennsylvania Infantry, then transferred at the same rank to the Veteran Reserve Corps. Later, he acted as assistant provost marshal in Trenton, New Jersey. Buried in Section F, Lot 787.

Brevet Brigadier General Clement A. Finley (1797–1879) graduated from the Medical School of the University of Pennsylvania in 1834 and entered the Regular Army, retiring as Surgeon General with the rank of colonel in 1862. Buried in Section I, Lot 168.

Mary Grew (1813–1896), abolitionist, suffragette, a founder of the Female Anti-Slavery Society.

Brevet Major General James Gwyn (1828–1906) was colonel of the 118th Pennsylvania. He was brevetted brigadier general for his services at the Battle of Poplar Spring Church (September 30, 1864), and to major general for the Battle of Five Forks (April 1, 1865). Buried in Section E, Lot 33.

Brevet Brigadier General Charles P. Herring (1829–1889) was lieutenant colonel of the 118th Pennsylvania. He was wounded at Hatcher's Run, Virginia, on February 6, 1865, losing his right leg as a result. Buried in Section M, Lot 85.

Brevet Brigadier General John Q. Lane (1831–1903) was colonel of the 97th Ohio. He moved east after the war and was a lawyer, passing away in Atlantic City, New Jersey. Buried in Section I, Lot 241.

Brevet Brigadier General James C. Lynch (1840–1901) first served in the 106th Pennsylvania, then on the staffs of Generals

Alexander Hays and John Gibbon. He then was commissioned colonel of the 183rd Pennsylvania. Buried in Section N, Lot 145.

Brevet Brigadier General Richard B. Price (1807–1876) was a member of the 1st City Troop and colonel of the 2nd Pennsylvania Cavalry. Buried in Section H, Lot 132.

Thomas A. Scott (1823–1881), Pennsylvania Railroad executive, was also Assistant Secretary of War during Lincoln's administration. Buried in Section M, Lot 3.

Emily Bliss Souder (1814–1886) was a volunteer nurse at Gettysburg who wrote a book about her experiences, *Leaves from the Battlefield of Gettysburg* (Philadelphia, 1864). Buried in Section F, Lot 348–349.

Brevet Brigadier General Charles H. Tay (1836–1871) was a colonel of the 18th New Jersey and promoted for gallantry and meritorious service. Buried in Section I, Lot 851.

Hours: Daily, 9 A.M. to 5 P.M. Tel. 215–386–2181.

Directions: From I–76 (Schuylkill Expressway), exit at South Street. Travel west on South Street (which becomes Spruce Street) to Thirty-eighth Street. Turn left on Thirty-eighth, then take first right turn below Spruce onto Baltimore Avenue. At light, continue straight ahead (Baltimore veers off to the right) onto Woodland Avenue. Go one block to Fortieth Street and turn left through cemetery gates.

OUTLYING SITES

BUCKS COUNTY HISTORICAL SOCIETY,
84 South Pine Street, Doylestown, PA 18901

The Bucks County Historical Society has a number of Civil War artifacts among its holdings. The primary item that can be viewed in the reading room is William Trego's massive painting *Rescue of the Colors*, which shows Hiram Purcell rescuing the colors of the 104th Pennsylvania during the Battle of Fair Oaks on May 31, 1862.

The Spruance Library is located on the Mercer Museum's third floor. Manuscript holdings include the following collections.

- ☞ Bucks County Volunteers. Collection, 1861–1865
- ☞ Burrill, John C. Journal, 1864. 196th PA
- ☞ Davis, William H. H. Papers, 1861–1865, Postwar. 104th PA
- ☞ Eisenbrey, J. Lehman. Journal, 1865. 16th PA Cavalry

- ☞ Ely, Albert S. Papers, 1863–1865. 20th PA Cavalry
- ☞ Ely, Samuel S. Diary, 1864. 20th PA Cavalry
- ☞ Fell, David N. Record Books. 122nd PA
- ☞ Grand Army of the Republic. Post 366 Records, 1883–1920
- ☞ Pennsylvania Infantry. 174th Regiment. Draft Records
- ☞ Purcell, Hiram W. Papers. 104th PA
- ☞ Torbert, Isaac L. Diary, 1862. 104th PA
- ☞ Widdifield, Caspar S. Papers. 84th PA

Hours: Mercer Museum: Monday–Saturday, 10 A.M. to 5 P.M.; Sunday, noon to 5 P.M. Spruance Library: Tuesday, 1 P.M. to 9 P.M.; Wednesday and Saturday, 10 A.M. to 5 P.M. Tel. 215–345–0210. Web site: www.mercermuseum.org. Admission fee: $5 for adults, $4.50 for senior citizens, $1.50 for children.

CHESTER COUNTY HISTORICAL SOCIETY, 225 North High Street, West Chester, PA 19380

The Chester County Historical Society has a sizable number of Civil War letters and diaries. (See the appendix for a listing of the major collections.) Keep in mind that this listing is by no means exhaustive, as the society also has many smaller collections not listed here.

Hours: Monday–Saturday, 9:30 A.M. to 4:30 P.M. Library schedule is the same except for Wednesday, when it is open from 1 P.M. to 8 P.M. Tel. 610–692–4800. Web site: www.chesterco-historical.org. Admission fee: $5 for adults, $4 for senior citizens, $2.50 for children age 6 to 17.

DELAWARE COUNTY HISTORICAL SOCIETY,
Room 208, Malin Road Center, Delaware County
Community College, Broomall, PA 19008

The Delaware County Historical Society is temporarily housed in a room on the campus of Delaware County Community College. As a result, its collection of artifacts is in temporary storage and unavailable for use. The library contains a few Civil War manuscript collections as well as the record books of two GAR posts: Wilde Post 25 and Bradbury Post 149.

Hours: Tuesday, 1 P.M. to 8 P.M.; Wednesday, 9 A.M. to 4 P.M. Tel. 610–359–1148. Web site: www.delcohistory.org/dchs. Admission fee: $3 for nonmembers.

DOYLESTOWN CEMETERY,
215 East Court Street, Doylestown, PA 18901

Two brevet brigadier generals are buried in this cemetery.

William H. H. Davis (1820–1910) was colonel of the 104th Pennsylvania and was awarded a brevet brigadier generalship in March 1865 for meritorious services during the siege operations at Charleston, South Carolina. Buried in Section K, Lot 56.

Horatio G. Sickel (1817–1890) was colonel of the 3rd Pennsylvania Reserves and then of the 198th Pennsylvania. He was brevetted brigadier general on October 21, 1864, for faithful and meritorious services, and brevetted major general in March 1865. Buried in Section B, Lot 7.

Hours: Daily during daylight hours; office is open Monday–Friday, 9 A.M. to 5 P.M. Tel. 215–348–3911.

FORT MIFFLIN, Fort Mifflin Road, Philadelphia, PA 19153

British troops began construction of this fort in 1772, but when war broke out, the Redcoats evacuated the unfinished site. The

FORT MIFFLIN

British returned in October 1777 and bombarded the fort for a month, forcing the outmanned garrison to evacuate on November 15. Following the War for Independence, the fort was reconstructed on plans designed by Pierre L'Enfant, the architect most famous for his design of Washington, D.C. During the Civil War, Fort Mifflin was used as a prison for mutinous Union soldiers.

Hours: 10 A.M. to 4 P.M. Tel. 215–492–1881. Admission fee: $6 for adults, $3 for senior citizens, $3 for children under 12 and students with ID, children under 5 free.

Directions: From I–95, exit at Island Avenue, go half a mile east to Fort Mifflin Road, then follow signs to the fort.

HISTORICAL SOCIETY OF MONTGOMERY COUNTY, 1654 DeKalb Street, Norristown, PA 1940

Located in an old mansion, the society has a number of Civil War artifacts among its holdings, including a flag of the 51st Pennsylvania, items taken from the Gettysburg wound of General Winfield S. Hancock, and the bullet Colonel William J. Bolton of the 51st Pennsylvania coughed up after the war. Owing to a lack of space, the society's holdings are at present largely unavailable for viewing. The society is raising money to build an addition to the present structure so that its holdings can be better stored and exhibited.

Among the society's Civil War manuscript holdings are the following collections.

☞ Ashenfelter, John H. Diary, 1864. 138th PA

☞ Bolton, William J. Postwar Scrapbooks. 51st PA

☞ Dalbey, Richard S. Letters, 1862, 1863. USS *Sabine*

☞ Denning, Joseph. Letters, 1861, 1864. 7th PA Cavalry

☞ Grand Army of the Republic. Records for Posts 11 (Zook), 79 (George Smith) and 515 (George B. McClellan)

☞ Hunsicker, Davis and Charles. Letters, 1861–1862. 51st PA

☞ Pennsylvania Infantry. 175th Regiment. Company A Books

☞ Schillich, John W. Diary, 1861–1865. 51st PA

☞ Woods, John W. Diary, 1864–1865. 20th PA Cavalry

Hours: Monday, Wednesday, Thursday, Friday, 10 A.M. to 4 P.M.; Tuesday, 1 P.M. to 9 P.M. Tel. 610–272–0297. Admission fee: $4 for nonmembers.

Directions: From the Pennsylvania Turnpike, exit at the Valley Forge Interchange (Exit 24) and proceed north on Route 202 into Norristown. Route 202 becomes the DeKalb Pike, and the historical society is on the right in the 1600 block.

HISTORICAL SOCIETY OF THE PHOENIXVILLE AREA, P.O. Box 552, Phoenixville, PA 19460

Located in the old Central Lutheran Church at the corner of Main and Church Streets, the society interprets the history of Phoenixville and the surrounding area. Of interest to Civil War buffs are several archival collections that include lists of area soldiers. The museum displays a model of the 3-inch ordnance rifle, a rifled artillery piece used during the Civil War. This type of cannon, invented by John Griffen in 1856, was manufactured at the Phoenix Iron Works, of which Griffen was superintendent. The company produced more than 1,400 of these "Griffen guns" during the war. Visitors to Phoenixville can see several full-sized originals on display in the town park.

HISTORICAL SOCIETY OF PHOENIXVILLE

THE GRIFFEN CANNON

ONE OF 1400 GUNS MADE AT PHOENIX
IRON COMPANY SHOPS BETWEEN 1860
AND 1865.

INVENTED BY JOHN GRIFFEN

THESE 3 INCH WROUGHT IRON RIFLED
FIELD PIECES SERVED THE UNION
FORCES WITH GREAT MERIT DURING
THE CIVIL WAR.

Hours: The museum is open on the first Sunday of every month from 1 P.M. to 4 P.M., and Wednesday–Friday, 9 A.M. to 3 P.M. The archive is open for research Wednesday–Friday, 9 A.M. to 3 P.M., but call ahead since the society is staffed entirely by volunteers. Tel. 610–935–7646. Admission fee: None.

LAWN VIEW CEMETERY,
500 Huntingdon Pike, Rockledge, PA 19046

The following brevet brigadier general is buried here.

DeWitt C. Baxter (1829–1881), colonel of the 72nd Pennsylvania (Baxter's Fire Zouaves), was brevetted brigadier general in March 1865 for bravery at Gettysburg and the Wilderness. Buried in Broad Lawn, Range 14, Grave 84.

Tel. 215–379–1600.

MONTGOMERY CEMETERY, Norristown

Civil War generals buried here include the following.

Winfield S. Hancock (1824–1886), was, simply put, perhaps the finest corps commander in the Union army during the Civil War. Born 11 miles north of Norristown, Hancock graduated from West Point in 1844. He was appointed a brigadier general in 1861 and led his brigade capably at Williamsburg, the Seven Days and Antietam. He was elevated to division command in the Second Corps and fought at Fredericksburg and Chancellorsville. At Gettysburg, Hancock led the Second Corps and was instrumental in winning the battle for the Union. Hancock led the corps at the Wilderness, Spotsylvania, Cold Harbor and Petersburg. In November 1864, his Gettysburg wound incapacitated him from further active command. Following the war,

MONTGOMERY CEMETERY OF NORRISTOWN

Hancock continued in the Regular Army and was the Democratic presidential candidate in 1880.

John F. Hartranft (1830–1889) entered the war as colonel of the 4th Pennsylvania, then organized and led the 51st Pennsylvania, which served with Burnside's Ninth Corps. Hartranft proved an extremely talented leader, and at times commanded a brigade and division in the corps before his appointment to brigadier general in May 1864. Following his division's recapture of Fort Stedman in March 1865, Hartranft was promoted to major general. He was placed in command of Old Capitol Prison and supervised the hanging of the Lincoln conspirators. After the war, Hartranft was twice elected governor of Pennsylvania. He was state National Guard commander as well.

Matthew R. McClennan (1834–1872), colonel of the 138th Pennsylvania, was brevetted brigadier general on April 2, 1865, for gallant and meritorious services before Petersburg.

Adam J. Slemmer (1829–1868) graduated from West Point in the class of 1850. When the war began, Lieutenant Slemmer was in command of the barracks at Pensacola, Florida. He moved the garrison to Fort Pickens and saved that fort for the Union. He was promoted to major of the newly organized 16th United States Infantry, which he led at the battle of Murfreesboro, Tennessee, where he was wounded severely and incapacitated for active service. Promoted to brigadier general, Slemmer held several administrative positions, then was sent to command Fort Laramie, Wyoming Territory, where he died of heart disease at age thirty-nine.

Samuel K. Zook (1821–1863) was born in Chester County, raised in Montgomery, then moved to New York, where he was superintendent of a telegraph company. In 1861, Zook was appointed colonel of the 57th New York, which he led until he was promoted to brigadier general in November 1862. His regiment and brigade were part of the Second Corps. At Gettysburg, Zook led his brigade into the Wheatfield, where he was mortally wounded, succumbing to his wound on July 3.

Hours: Montgomery Cemetery is managed by the Historical Society of Montgomery County. Tel. 610–272–0297 for details and accessibility.

OAKLANDS CEMETERY, West Chester,
c/o William Wood Company,
120 West Market Street, West Chester, PA 19382

The following brevet generals are buried here:

Henry R. Guss (1825–1907), colonel of the 97th Pennsylvania, was brevetted brigadier general and major general in March 1865 for gallant and meritorious services. Buried in Section F, Lot 28.

William L. James (1833–1903) became a colonel in the quartermaster corps and served as Chief Quartermaster of the Department of Virginia. He was brevetted brigadier general on March 1, 1866, for faithful and meritorious services. Buried in Section D, Lot 12.

Hours: Oaklands Cemetery is located on Route 100 (the Pottstown Pike), and is managed by the William Wood Company. Please call for information on visiting the cemetery. Tel. 610–692–3966.

RIVERSIDE CEMETERY, 200 South Montgomery Avenue,
Norristown, PA 19403

The following brevet brigadier general is buried in this cemetery:

William J. Bolton (1833–1906) was colonel of the 51st Pennsylvania and brevetted brigadier general in March 1865 for gallant and meritorious services. Buried in Central Lawn, Lot 159.

Hours: The cemetery is open during daylight hours, while the office is open Monday–Friday, 10 A.M. to 5 P.M. Tel. 610–539–1073.

Lodging in the Area

For travelers wishing to stay in buildings that existed during the 1860s, there are several bed and breakfast agencies that list historic homes from this period. Advance reservations are a must for most bed and breakfasts. Call the numbers listed for details on prices, locations and other pertinent information.

**Bed & Breakfast, Center City,
1804 Pine Street,
Philadelphia, PA 19103**

Headquartered across the street from the Civil War Library and Museum, this organization lists dozens of hosts in and around center city Philadelphia. See their web site for more details on prices and accommodations.

Tel. 215–735–1137. Web site: www.centercitybed.com.

**Bed & Breakfast Connections of Philadelphia,
P.O. Box 21, Devon, PA 19333**

Mary Alice Hamilton has more than fifty hosts lined up to receive guests. Among the Civil War period homes are the following.

- ☞ 1807 townhouse located at Fourth and Spruce Streets
- ☞ 1811 brick townhouse located at Front and Lombard Streets

- ☞ Colonial Garden, a combination of three colonial houses located at Fourth and Bainbridge Streets
- ☞ 1836 townhouse at Tenth and Clinton Streets
- ☞ 1800s townhouse at Twelfth and Pine Streets
- ☞ 1846 federal townhouse at Thirteenth and Lombard Streets
- ☞ 1860s house at Twenty-first and Cypress Streets
- ☞ Nineteenth-century bank barn on the Main Line
- ☞ 1780s house in East Falls

Tel. 610–687–3565; 800–448–3619. Web site: www.bnbphiladelphia.com.

Also, visit the City of Philadelphia's web site to view additional information about area accommodations at www.libertynet.com.

Appendix

Selected List of Philadelphia Businesses
That Received Government Contracts
During the Civil War

Listed are the major businesses that obtained government contracts from the years 1861–1865. Included is name of business, location (primary location if business changed locale during the war) and primary types of goods supplied.

Name	Location	Goods Supplied
Adolph & Keen	62 N. 2nd	hats
Anspach & Stanton	122 N. 3rd	clothing
Arnold, Nysbaum & Nirdling	55 N. 3rd	trousers
Bailey & Co.	819 Chestnut	swords
Charles P. Bayard	720 S. 5th	haversacks
Leonard S. Beals	132 S. 3rd	insignia
Martin Bellows		shoes
Berg, Leon & Co.	426–28 Market	clothing
Bloomingdale & Rhine	332 Market	greatcoats
David B. Bowser	481 N. 4th	artist (flags)
Samuel Brewer	11 S. 3rd	artist (flags)
Henry C. Brolaskey	108 S. 13th	clothing
Matthew Brooks	139 N. 3rd	caps

Name	Location	Goods Supplied
Brooks & Co.	41 N. 3rd	caps
Burkert & Koedel		shoes
Charles Burnham	117 S. 10th	tinware
Robert D. Clifton	203 S. 2nd	clothing
Code, Hopper & Co.	1502 Filbert	canteens
William Y. Colladay	245 Market	clothing
William B. Cozens	241 Chestnut	tents
William C. Dare	21 N. 2nd	hats
Dexter, Lambert & Co.	219 Chestnut	tassels, cords, chevrons
L. Dickerman & Co.		shoes
Henry Disston & Sons	62–69 Laurel	swords
L. B. M. Dolby	South Delaware Avenue	tent poles, knapsacks
Albert Dorff	1528 Callowhill	canteens
William Dunlap	428 S. 13th	clothing
Henry Eggeling & Co.	309 Race	drumsticks, fifes
J. Henry Ehrlicher	321 N. 3rd	uniforms
Emons & Marshall		swords
D. C. Enos		shoes
Benjamin C. Evans & Co.	246 Walnut	trousers
Evans & Hassall	418 Arch	flags
John W. Everman	103 James Alley	haversacks, tents
John A. Evers		shoes
Paul J. Field	747 S. 2nd	axes, hatchets
Henry L. Foster	111 N. Delaware	clothing
John C. Fuller	40 S. 3rd	buttons, sashes
Goldthorp, Woodward & Co.	625 Market	tassels, hat cords
John C. Graham	525 Cherry	uniforms
Robert H. Gratz	214 N. 19th	canteens
William H. Gray	627 Arch	insignia
Hadden, Booth & Porter	130 N. 2nd	canteens
Henry G. Haedrich	237 S. 15th	accoutrements

Name	Location	Goods Supplied
Samuel Hall	1326 Green	insignia
Charles Hallowell		shoes
Charles Hammond	528 Commerce	axes
William S. Hansel & Sons	114 Market	accoutrements, saddles
Harkness Brothers	338 Market	clothing
R. P. Harmer	927 Market	accoutrements
Harvey & Ford	422 Library	slings, snares
Hazel & Co.		shoes
William T. Hellerman		shoes
Henry W. Hensel	20 N. 4th	sashes, trim
Philip Hill	259 Market	buttons
Hood, Bunright & Co.		uniforms, buttons
Horstmann Brothers & Co.	5th and Cherry	swords, uniforms, flags, buttons, insignia
F. & N. Jones		shoes
D. R. King & Co.		shoes
David Klein	918 Market	military tailors
F. A. Klemm & Brother	705 Market	bugles
J. H. Krider		weapons
Kunkle, Hall & Co.	525 Market	clothing
Charles Laing & Co.	6th and Chestnut	hats
Lambert & Mast	532 Callowhill	sashes, caps
Joseph Lamberti	226 Dock	caps
Alexander T. Lane	419 Market	clothing
Lesley & Co.	611 Market	drums, ferrules
Levick & Rasin	505 Market	ponchos, rubber blankets, shoes
Lewis, Wharton & Boardman	238 Chestnut	clothing, tents
Thomas R. Little	134 Green	box/belt plates
Michael Magee & Co.	18 Decatur	saddles
F. J. Magill	10 Walnut	canteens

Name	Location	Goods Supplied
William H. McRae		shoes
Emanuel Metzger	605 Arch	halters, scabbards, cap pouches, ammunition boxes
John M. Migeod	27 S. 8th	sword belts, holsters, cartridge boxes, bridles, saddle cloths, medical saddle bags
William G. Mintzer	131 N. 3rd	buttons
Morgan & Walbank	204 Walnut	drum heads
E. P. Moyer & Brothers	220 Market	leather goods, plates
William Muldoon		shoes
John Mundell		shoes
W. J. Murphy & Co.		shoes
James Naulty	459–61 Dillwyn	accoutrements
Nece, Reuben & Co.	1110 Noble	accoutrements
Joseph Newhouse	822 Market	clothing
Charles Oakford & Son	828–30 Chestnut	hats
Abraham Oppenheimer	517 Market	hat cords, engineer overalls, tents
Charles H. Owens		shoes
Joseph F. Page	114/237 Market	clothing
William H. Pearce	33–35 S. 8th	accoutrements
T. Morris Perotand Co.	314 Vine	mess chests
Samuel R. Phillips	30–32 S. 7th	accoutrements
Thomas Potter	229 Arch	knapsacks, haversacks, ponchos, blankets

Name	Location	Goods Supplied
James W. Queen & Co.	924 Chestnut	signal telescopes
George Raphael	109 South Front	weapons importer
Jacob Reed	301–5 S. 2nd	clothing
Ridgeway & Rufe	Germantown	bayonets
Charles C. Roberts	400 Market	knapsacks, tents
H. Robinson & Co.		blankets
Rockhill & Wilson	603–5 Chestnut	uniforms
Joseph H. Rohrman	606–10 Cherry	canteens
F. J. Rosenberg	422 N. 4th	clothing
William F. Scheible	49 S. 3rd	flags, tents
Joseph Schilling	993 N. 7th	swords
T. & E. Schliefflin		swords
Henry W. Scott	533–35 Market	clothing
Sheble & Fisher	3 N. 5th	swords
George W. Simons	610 Sansom	swords
Slade, Smith & Co.	40–42 South Front	clothing
Joseph F. Smith	1737 Arch	shoes, ponchos
Smith, Williams & Co.	513 Market	clothing
Snyder & Co.		felt hats
Soistman Family	458 Dillwyn	drums
Stanton, Mayer & Frank	126 N. 3rd	clothing
William C. Stiles	22nd and Arch	canteens
D. J. Sutherland	120 S. 17th	accoutrements, kettles, mess pans
E. Tracy	524 Cherry	clothing, haversacks
George W. Tryon	Germantown	knives
Ernest Vogt	235 Beaver	drums
Samuel D. Walton & Co.	125 N. 3rd	caps
Wanamaker & Brown	6th and Market	buttons

Name	Location	Goods Supplied
Benjamin Warden	922 Filbert	accoutrements
Henry Wilson	715 S. 6th	insignia
William P. Wilstach & Co.	38 N. 3rd	insignia
Worman, Ely & Co.	118th N. 3rd	knife–fork–spoon combo
Wright Brothers & Co.	322–24 Market	trousers
William M. Yomer	426 Wharton	clothing
Charles M. Zimmerman	238 N. 2nd	drums

Military Hospitals in Philadelphia, 1861–1865

Broad Street General Hospital, 650 beds, southeast corner of Broad and Cherry Streets. Opened February 1862 in the old Philadelphia and Reading Railroad Station. Branches later were opened in the market house on Broad Street below Race Street and on Cherry Street east of Broad. Patients moved to Mower General Hospital when that establishment opened.

Catharine Street Hospital, 105 beds, Eighth and Catharine Streets.

Christian Street Hospital, 220 beds, Ninth and Christian Streets. Located in Moyamensing Hall. Open until October 1864.

Citizens' Volunteer Hospital, 400 beds, northeast corner of Broad and Prime Streets. Located opposite the depot of the Philadelphia, Wilmington and Baltimore Railroad. Open from September 1862 to August 1865.

Cuyler General Hospital, 550 beds, Germantown, located in the rear of Town Hall. Opened September 1862.

Episcopal General Hospital, 325 beds, Front and York Streets.

Fifth Street Hospital, 282 beds, Fifth and Buttonwood Streets, in the Dunlap Carriage Factory buildings. Open from February 1862 to February 1863. Location then used as a prison for captured Confederates and as barracks for city Provost Guard.

Filbert Street Hospital, 430 beds, southeast corner of Sixteenth and Filbert

Streets. Located in State Armory building. Began in the summer of 1862; by February 1863, this hospital had become a convalescent site.

George Street Hospital, 225 beds, Fourth and George Streets. Located in the building used by the Order of American Mechanics. In operation from June 1862 to February 1863.

Haddington General Hospital, 200 beds, Sixty-fifth and Vine Streets, in the Bull's Head Tavern. In operation from November 1862 to about November 1863.

Hestonville General Hospital, 172 beds.

Master Street Hospital, 305 beds, Sixth and Master Streets. Located in a manufacturing building on the northwest corner. Opened July 1862 and closed after Mower General Hospital opened.

McClellan General Hospital, 400 beds, Germantown Road and Cayuga Street.

Mower General Hospital, 4,000 beds, Chestnut Hill, along the track of the Reading Railroad and bounded by Abington and Springfield Avenues. Largest military hospital in the city, opened in January 1863.

Officers' General Hospital, 50 beds, Camac's Woods, near intersection of Eleventh and Berks Streets. Opened in November 1862. Late in the war this hospital was moved to Twenty-fourth and Chestnut Streets.

Race Street Hospital, 412 beds, located in National Guards' Armory. Open until March 1863.

St. Joseph's Hospital, 150 beds, Seventeenth Street and Girard Avenue. Located in temporary wooden buildings erected on the grounds of St. Joseph's.

Satterlee General Hospital, 2,860 beds, located in west Philadelphia, from Baltimore Avenue to Pine Street, and bounded also by Forty-third and forty-sixth Streets. Opened in June 1862, closed on August 3, 1865. Shelter tents erected on hospital grounds provided space for 900 additional beds.

Smallpox General Hospital, 50 beds, Islington Lane.

South Street Hospital, 253 beds, Twenty-fourth and South Streets.

Summit House General Hospital, 522 beds, Darby Road near Paschalville in West Philadelphia. In August 1864, the white patients at Summit were removed to Satterlee to make room for sick and wounded black soldiers. Later, St. Joseph's Catholic Hospital was built on this site.

Turner's Lane General Hospital, 275 beds, Twenty-second and Oxford Streets.

Twelfth Street Hospital, 152 beds, Twelfth and Buttonwood Streets. Opened in October 1862 for about a year.

Wood Street Hospital, 175 beds, Twenty-second and Wood Streets. Open until February 1863, when patients were transferred to Mower General Hospital.

Civil War Manuscript Collections in the Historical Society of Pennsylvania

Alloway, John W. 1863 Diary. Battery B, 1st PA Artillery.

Antediluvian Society Infants' Clothing Association. Papers.

Ashhurst, Lewis and Mary. Diaries, 1861–1865. Civilians.

Baker, Enoch T. Letters, 1861–1862. 110th PA.

Barr, John P. Diaries, August 1861–May 1865. 4th PA Cavalry.

Benners, Henry. Diaries. Glass manufacturer.

Bennett, Frank T. Diary, 1862. 55th PA.

Betts, Charles M. Papers. 15th PA Cavalry.

Biddle, William F. Papers. Aide to General William B. McClellan.

Boos, Louis J. Personal Reminiscence. 6th PA Cavalry. In Civil War Papers Collection.

Brooke, John R. Papers. Colonel, 53rd PA. General officer.

Cavada, Adolfo. Diary, April 1861–December 1863. Aide to General Andrew A. Humphreys.

Clark, Thomas. Letters, 1864. 97th PA.

Clay, Cecil. Papers. 58th PA.

Clymer, Meredith. Letters. U.S. Surgeon.

Congdon, James A. Letters, 1862–1865. 12th PA Cavalry.

Cornett, J. A. Letters, 1861–1865. 5th PA Cavalry. In Jane Cornett Papers.

Cornett, Joseph. Letters, November 1862–May 1863. 176th PA. Letters, October 1864–June 1865. 199th PA. In Jane Cornett Papers.

Diller, W. S. Papers. 76th PA.

Dougherty, Daniel. Diary, 1863–1864. 63rd PA.

Fahnestock, George W. Diaries. Wealthy drug merchant.

Foering, John O. Papers. 28th PA.

Fox, Isaac. Papers. 114th PA.

Furness, Horace. Papers. Includes extensive material on 1864 Sanitary Fair.

Gibbon, John. Letters. General officer.

Griffith, Richard. Diaries, 1862–1863. 23rd PA. In Mrs. Irvin H. Mckesson Papers.

Harrison, Joseph. Letterbook. Businessman.

Humphreys, Andrew A. Papers. General officer.

Irvin, John. Diaries, 1863–1865. 149th PA.

Israel, W. P. Letters, 1861–1862. 1st OH Artillery.

Johnson, Jesse. Diary, July 1862–April 1863. 7th WV.

Johnson, Private. Diary, November 1861–July 1864. WV Cavalry Company from Fayette County, PA.

Jones, D. D. Papers. 88th PA. In Civil War Papers Collection.

Jones, Owen. Letters, 1861–1863. 1st PA Cavalry. In Jones Family Papers.

Jones, William T. Reminiscences. 61st PA.

Jordan, Thomas J. Papers. 9th PA Cavalry.

Justice, Jefferson. Papers. 100th PA.

Kappler, Jacob C. Letters. 99th PA.

Kendig, Abraham. Letters, November 1861–May 1864. 97th PA.

Kendig, Henry. Letters, December 1861–August 1863. 97th PA.

Lee, George F. Letters. Businessman.

Lynch, J. W. Letters. 106th PA.

MacManus, Susan T. Diaries. Civilian.

Magdalen Society of Philadelphia. Papers.

Manley, W. H. Letters, September 1861–May 1862. 72nd PA.

Margerum, Richard. Letters, August 1861–January 1864. 71st PA.

Markley, John H. Diary, August 1862–November 1863. 138th PA. In Dreer Collection.

McAteer, Simon. Diary, 1864. 12th PA Cavalry.

McCall, George A. Papers. General officer.

McCarter, William. Reminiscences, 1862. 116th PA.

Meade, George G. Papers. General officer.

Newhall, W. S. Papers. 3rd PA Cavalry.

Norris, Henry P. Letters, 1861–1862. U.S. Artillery.

Pennsylvania Infantry. 29th Regiment. Collection.

Pennsylvania Infantry. 36th Infantry (7th Reserves). Company G Books. In
    Civil War Papers Collection.

Pennsylvania Infantry. 52nd Regiment. Collection.

Pennsylvania Infantry. 96th Regiment. Company G Rolls. In Civil War
    Papers Collection.

Penrose, Washington. Diaries. Pattern maker.

Rawle, William B. Papers. 3rd PA Cavalry. In Rawle Family Papers.

Reed, William W. Diary, August 2–October 16, 1862. 127th PA.

Seckel, Edwin R. W. Scattered Letters, 1861–1864. 51st PA.

Sickel, Horatio G. Postwar Letters. 3rd PA Reserves. In Ungar Collection.

Smith, John L. Papers. 118th PA.

Smith, Thomas W. Letters. 6th PA Cavalry.

Smoyer, E. B. Letters. 1st PA Cavalry.

Spehlman, B. F. Papers. 122nd PA, 1st PA Artillery.

Stackhouse, William. Diaries. 119th PA.

Thatcher, Isaac S. Letters. 8th NJ.

Truefitt, Henry P. Papers. 119th PA. In Gratz Collection.

Union Benevolent Association. Papers.

Union Volunteer Refreshment Saloon. Papers.

Voltaire, Louis. Papers. 98th PA. In Civil War Papers Collection.

Wallen, Augustus B.

Wenrick, James E. Diary, April–October 1864. 19th PA Cavalry.

Wharton, Katherine B. Diaries. Civilian.

Williamson, Peter. Papers. Civilian.

Winner, Septunius. Diaries. Civilian.

Civil War Manuscripts Collections in the Chester County Historical Society

Bell, Thomas S. Papers, 1861–1862. 51st PA.

Blakeslee, William R. Diaries, 1862–1863. 115th PA.

Brinton, Daniel G. Letters, 1863–1864. Surgeon.

Bull, S. O. Letters, 1862–1865. 53rd PA.

Christman, E. L. Letters, 1861–1863. 4th PA Reserves.

Darlington, Joseph. Papers, 1861–1864. 1st PA Reserves.

Darlington, William H. Letters, 1861. 1st PA Reserves.

Dean, John. Diary, 1862. 97th PA.

Durnall, Joel B. Diary, 1864. 192nd PA.

Guss, Francis M. Papers. 97th PA.

Hannum, Norris M. Diaries, 1862–1863. 1862 PA Militia Cavalry.

Hayes, Lewis D. Letters, 1864–1865. 97th PA.

Kendig, Abraham. Letters, 1861–1864. 97th PA.

Leech, William A. Letters, 1862–1865. 90th PA.

McCauley, Levi G. Diary, 1862. 7th PA Reserves.

Mercer, Eber T. Letters, 1861–1865. 29th PA.

Pennsylvania Infantry. 30th Regiment (1st Reserves). Companies C and E Books.

Pennsylvania Infantry. 97th Regiment. Company A Books. In Reunion Society Papers.

Pennsylvania Infantry. 124th Regiment. Company A Books. In Reunion Society Papers.

Pennsylvania Infantry. 192nd Regiment. Company P Books.

Pennypacker, Galusha. Letters, 1862–1865. 97th PA.

Pennypacker, Nathan A. Letters, 1861–1864. 4th PA Reserves.

Price, Rebecca. Manuscript Recollections. Nurse.

Price, William H. Letters, 1862–1864. U.S. Navy.

Rupert, Alfred. Letters, 1861–1865. 1st PA Reserves.

Sheaff, C. S. Letters, 1861–1862. 1st PA Reserves.

Speakman, Charles. Letters. 1st PA Reserves.
Taggart, John H. Letters, 1863–1865. Free Military School, USCT.
Turner, John P. Company A History. 1st PA Reserves.
Turner, William H. Diaries, 1862–1864. 1st PA Reserves.
Way, Joseph. Letters, 1861–1864. 1st PA Reserves.
Way, William J. Letters, 1862–1864. 1st PA Reserves.

Philadelphia Shipyards and Their Vessels

The Philadelphia Naval Yard and the larger Cramp's Shipyard were the two largest yards located on the Delaware River. Others in existence during the Civil War were the following:

- ☞ Jacob Birely & John W. Lynn, Kensington area

- ☞ Hillman & Streaker, Kensington area

- ☞ Merrick & Sons, Southwark area

- ☞ Neafie & Levy, located near Cramp's (1838–1907)

- ☞ Reany, Son & Archbold, Chester (1859–1871)

- ☞ Vaughan & Fisher, Kensington area (1851–1863)

The ships built in Philadelphia during the war are listed as follows:

Ship Name	Type	Launched	Yard
Alligator	Submarine	April 30, 1862	Neafie
Arkansas	Bark	June 27, 1863	Cramp
Carnation	Screw Tug	August 17, 1863	Neafie
Chattanooga	Screw Sloop	October 13, 1864	Cramp
Emerald	Yacht	August 3, 1864	Neafie
Epsilon	Screw Tug	June 3, 1864	Neafie
Glance	Screw Tug	June 2, 1864	Reany
Itasca	Screw Gunboat	October 1, 1861	Hillman & Streaker

Ship Name	Type	Launched	Yard
Juniata	Screw Sloop	March 20, 1862	U.S.
Kansas	Screw Gunboat	September 29, 1863	U.S.
Lehigh	Monitor, 2 turrets	January 17, 1863	Reany
Miami	Sidewheel Gunboat	November 16, 1861	U.S.
Monongahela	Screw Sloop	July 10, 1862	U.S.
New Ironsides	Armored Vessel	May 10, 1862	Cramp
Nina	Steam Tug	May 27, 1865	Reany
Periwinkle	Screw Tug	December 9, 1864	Neafie
Pinta	Steam Tug	October 29, 1864	Reany
Pontiac	Sidewheel Gunboat	1863	Hillman & Streaker
Sangamon	Monitor, 2 turrets	October 27, 1862	Reany
Sciota	Screw Gunboat	October 15, 1861	Birely
Shamokin	Sidewheel Gunboat	1864	Reany
Shenandoah	Screw Sloop	December 8, 1862	U.S.
Suwanee	Sidewheel Gunboat	March 13, 1864	Reany
Swatara	Screw Gunboat	May 23, 1865	U.S.
Tacony	Sidewheel Gunboat	May 7, 1863	U.S.
Tonawanda	Monitor, 2 turrets	May 6, 1864	U.S.
Tunxis	Monitor, 2 turrets	June 4, 1864	Reany
Tuscarora	Screw Sloop	August 24, 1861	U.S.
Wateree	Sidewheel Gunboat	August 29, 1863	Reany
Wissahickon	Screw Gunboat	October 2, 1861	John W. Lynn
Wyalusing	Sidewheel Gunboat	May 12, 1863	Cramp
Yantic	Screw Gunboat	March 19, 1864	U.S.
Yazoo	Monitor, 2 turrets	May 8, 1865	Cramp

Philadelphia Businesses That Received
Government Ordnance Contracts During the Civil War

Name	Dates	Goods Supplied	Contract Value ($)
Bailey & Co., 819 Chestnut	1863	Enfield rifles	3,881.80
Isaac Broome, 108 S. 3rd	1861	cavalry lances	6,006.00
Chase, Sharpe & Thompson, 209 N. 2nd	1863–64	artillery projectiles	6,516.00
Dickson & Zane	1864	artillery projectiles	33,216.60
Joseph C. Grubb & Co., 236 Market	1861–62	sabers, carbines, pistols	67,002.95
Henry Holthausen, 221 Chestnut	1861–62	French muskets	524,015.47
Horstmann Brothers & Co.	1861–64	sabers, swords	140,245.25
Alfred Jenks & Son, 65–67 N. Front, Bridesburg	1861–65	rifle muskets	1,959,537.20
Philip S. Justice, 14 N. 5th	1861–62	rifles, pistols, swords	311,975.55
Henry G. Leisenring, 132 S. 3rd	1861	cavalry sabers	148,372.00
North, Chase & North, 209 N. 2nd	1861–63	artillery projectiles	184,687.76
Phoenix Iron Works, 410 Walnut (office)	1861–64	3-inch ordnance rifles	347,374.80
John Pondir, 221 Chestnut	1861–63	rifle muskets	703,208.19
Richardson & Overman, 1255 N. 12th	1861–65	Gallagher's carbines	506,270.00
Savery & Co., Front & Reed	1864–65	artillery projectiles	188,243.89
Sharp & Hanks	1862–63	Sharp's carbines	36,845.00
William P. Wilstach & Co., 38 N. 3rd	1861	sabers and swords	10,622.00

Total contracts   **$5,178,020.20**

Pennsylvania Troops Recruited in Philadelphia

The following is a list of companies raised in Philadelphia during the Civil War, organized by regiment. Included are company nicknames, when known, in parentheses. Infantry regiments had ten companies, lettered A–K; but sometimes a regiment might contain twelve or fifteen companies. Cavalry and Artillery regiments had twelve companies, the last two of which were lettered L and M.

17th Infantry (Quaker Regiment)
Entire Regiment, Companies A–K
- A (Washington Greys)
- B (Philadelphia Greys)
- C (West Philadelphia Greys)
- D (National Artillery)
- E (State Guard)
- F (2nd Company Washington Greys)
- G (2nd Company Philadelphia Greys)
- H (Cadwalader Greys)
- I (Independent Greys)
- K (2nd Company Cadwalader Greys)

18th Infantry
Entire Regiment, Companies A–K
- A (2nd Company Washington Blues)
- B (1st Company National Greys)
- C (Garde Lafayette)
- D (Philadelphia Zouaves)
- E (1st Company State Fencibles)
- F (1st Company Washington Blues)
- G (Minute Men of '76)
- H (2nd Company National Greys)
- I (Voltigeurs)
- K (2nd Company State Fencibles)

19th Infantry (National Guards)
Entire Regiment, Companies A–K

20th Infantry (Scott Legion)
Entire Regiment, Companies A–K

21st Infantry (German Rifle Regiment)
Entire Regiment, Companies A–K
- A (Jackson Rifles)
- B (Lafayette Rifles)
- C (Pennsylvania Rifles)
- D (Washington Rifles)
- E (Black Rifles)
- F (Steuben Rifles)
- G (Philadelphia Rifles)
- H (DeKalb Rifles)
- I (Scott Rifles)
- K (Franklin Rifles)

22nd Infantry (Philadelphia Light Guards Regiment)
Entire Regiment, Companies A–K
- I (Wheatley Guards)

23rd Infantry (3 months)
Entire Regiment, Companies A–K
- A (Continental Guards)

23rd Infantry (3 years)
Companies A–K, M, O, P, R
- B (Gymnast Zouaves)
- K (2nd Company Gymnast Zouaves)
- O (Independent Grays)

24th Infantry (Irish Regiment)
Companies A–G, I, K
- A (Irish Volunteers)
- B (Hibernia Greens)
- C (Emmett Guards)
- D (Meagher Guards)
- E (Jackson Guards)
- F (1st Company Shields Guards)
- G (Patterson Light Guards)
- I (2nd Company Shields Guards)

26th Infantry
Entire Regiment, Companies A–K
- A (Washington Guards)
- B (Anderson Guards)
- C (1st Company Monroe Guards)
- D (4th Company Monroe Guards)
- E (Union Invincibles)
- F (Cameron Guards)
- G (2nd Company Monroe Guards)
- H (3rd Company Monroe Guards)

- I (2nd Company Frankford Guards)
- K (1st Company Frankford Guards)

27th Infantry
Entire Regiment, Companies A–K
- F (Harrison Guards)

28th Infantry
Companies C, D, I, K, M, P
- C (Geary Guards)
- D (2nd Company Independent Grays)
- I (Gorgas Light Guard)
- K (Rover Guards)
- M (Union Grays)
- P (Scott Legion)

29th Infantry
Entire Regiment, Companies A–K
- A (Marion Guards)
- B (2nd Company West Philadelphia Grays)
- C (United Rifles)
- D (Koska Guards)
- E (Belmont Guards)
- F (Warren Guards)
- G (Federal Guard)
- H (Henry Clay Invincibles)
- I (Morgan Artillery)
- K (Dougherty Guards)

31st Infantry (2nd Reserves)
Entire Regiment, Companies A–K
- A (Penn Rifles)
- B (Governor's Rangers)

C (Hibernian Target Company)
D (Governor's Rangers)
E (Scotch Rifles)
F (Governor's Rangers)
G (Taggart Guards)
H (Independent Rangers)
I (Constitution Rangers)
K (Consolidation Guards)
B (replacement company)

32nd Infantry (3rd Reserves)
E (DeSilver Greys)
G (Germantown Guards)
K (Ontario Infantry)

33rd Infantry (4th Reserves)
A (Able Guards)
B (Quaker City Guards)
D (Dickson Guards)
G (Harmer Guards)
I (Reed Guards)

36th Infantry (7th Reserves)
E (Ridgway Guards)
G (2nd Philadelphia Guards)
K (Douglas Guards)

41st Infantry (12th Reserves)
A (Wayne Guards)

43rd Regiment (1st Artillery)
C (Flying Artillery)
D (Richmond Artillerists)
G (McCall Artillery)
H (Brady's Artillery)

56th Infantry
Portions of Companies D and I

58th Infantry
Companies A, B, C, D, K

59th Regiment (2nd Cavalry)
Companies B, C, E, G, part of K

60th Regiment (3rd Cavalry)
Companies A, B, C, E, F, I, K, M
A (Philadelphia Merchant Troop)

61st Infantry
Company I
G (Lyon Guards)
H (Marshall Guards)

65th Regiment (5th Cavalry)
Companies A–K

67th Infantry
Company I
B (Schuylkill Rangers)
E (part)

68th Infantry (Scott Legion)
Entire Regiment, Companies A–K

69th Infantry
Entire Regiment, Companies A–K
A (Irish Volunteers)
C (Emmett Guards)
D (Montgomery Guards)
G (Montgomery Guards)
I (Tiger Zouaves)
K (Independent Guards)

70th Regiment (6th Cavalry)
(Rush's Lancers)
Companies A–F, H–M

71st Infantry (California Regiment)
Companies A–G, M, N, P, parts of H, I, K
C (Pennsylvania Guards)
F (Spring Garden Minie Rifles)

72nd Infantry (Baxter's Fire Zouaves)
Entire Regiment, Companies A–K, L, M, N, P, R
    E (Ellsworth Zouaves)
    L (Keystone Guards)

73rd Infantry (Pennsylvania Legion)
Entire Regiment, Companies A–K
    B (Read Guards)

74th Infantry
    Company A, part of K

75th Infantry
Entire Regiment, Companies A–K

80th Regiment (7th Cavalry)
Part of Company F

81st Infantry
Companies A–F
    F (2nd Company Cadwalader Greys)

82nd Infantry
Companies A, C–K
    D (2nd Company Garde Lafayette)
    H (Greble Guards)

88th Infantry
Companies C–G, I, K
    F (Montgomery Guards)

89th Regiment (8th Cavalry)
    Companies C–L

90th Infantry (National Guards)
Entire Regiment, Companies A–K

91st Infantry

Entire Regiment, Companies A–K
    I (Union Guards)

95th Infantry (Gosline's Zouaves)
Companies A, C–K, replacement Companies F and I

98th Infantry
Entire Regiment, Companies A–K

99th Infantry
Companies A–K
    G (Union Zouaves)
    I (Jackson Zouaves)

104th Infantry
Part of Company I

106th Infantry
Companies A–E, G, H, I, K

108th Regiment (11th Cavalry)
Company C

109th Infantry (Curtin Light Guard)
Companies A–C, E–K

110th Infantry
Companies E, F, G, H, I
    E (Dare Guards)
    F (Scott Fusiliers)
    G (Lewis Guards)
    H (Fitz Greys)
    I (Henry Guards)

112th Regiment (2nd Heavy Artillery)
Companies A–I contained many Philadelphians in each company, and contingents from many other counties

113th Regiment (12th Cavalry)
Companies A, C, parts of D and I

114th Infantry (Collis' Zouaves)
Entire Regiment, Companies A–K
   A (Zouaves d'Afrique)
   C (Cooper's Guard)

115th Infantry
Companies A, B, C, E, F, H, I, K
   A (Jackson Guards)
   B (Hibernia Greens)
   C (Patterson Light Guards)
   F (Shields Guards)

116th Infantry
Entire Regiment, Companies A–K,
replacement Company E

117th Regiment (13th Cavalry)
   Companies A–D, H–M

118th Infantry (Corn Exchange
Regiment)
Entire Regiment, Companies A–K

119th Infantry
Companies A–D, F, G, I, K

121st Infantry
Companies B–E, G–K

147th Infantry
Companies M and P (28th Infantry)
became Companies D and E
   I (Schuylkill Arsenal Guard)

150th Infantry
Companies A, B, E, F

152nd Regiment (3rd Heavy
Artillery)
Companies A–C, E–M

154th Infantry
Companies A, B, C

157th Infantry
Companies A–D

159th Regiment (14th Cavalry)
   A (Washington Cavalry)

160th Regiment (15th Cavalry)
Companies B and L, and parts of A,
C, D, E, G, H, I, M

161st Regiment (16th Cavalry)
   I (Russell Troop)

162nd Regiment (17th Cavalry)
Part of Company I

163rd Regiment (18th Cavalry)
Company M, part of Company L

174th Infantry
Part of Company I

179th Infantry
Parts of Companies A, C, G

180th Regiment (19th Cavalry)
Companies A–K

181st Regiment (20th Cavalry)
Companies B, C, G, K, part of
Company M (6 months); Companies C, F, G, H, and parts of Companies D, I, M
(3 years)

182nd Regiment (21st Cavalry)
Part of Company M

183rd Infantry (4th Union
League)
Entire Regiment, Companies A–K

186th Infantry
Entire Regiment, Companies A–K

187th Infantry
Company E, parts of Companies F
and K

192nd Infantry
Companies A–M, P (3 months);
Company E (1 year)

196th Infantry (5th Union
League)
Companies A–D, F–K

197th Infantry (3rd Coal
Exchange)
Companies B, D, E, H, K
   K (Courtland Saunders
      Minute Men)

198th Infantry (6th Union
League)
Companies A, B, C, E, F, I, K, L, O
   C (Saunders Guards)

199th Infantry (Commercial Regiment)
Companies B, D, E, parts of Companies A, C, G, H

203rd Infantry (Birney's Sharp-
shooters)
Part of Company D

213th Infantry (7th Union League)
Companies A, B, C, E, H, parts of
Companies F, G, I, K

214th Infantry (8th Union
League)
Companies A, D, E, F, G, I, K, part
of Company C

215th Infantry (9th Union
League)
Company K, parts of Companies
A, C, D, E, F, G, H, I

Independent Battery A

Part of Independent Battery E

Keystone Battery

1st City Troop (1861 and 1863)

**Gaskill's Independent Company of
Engineers**

Chestnut Hill Hospital Company

1862 Militia

7th Regiment (Gray Reserves)
Entire Regiment, Companies A–K
   L (Starr's Battery)

8th Regiment (2nd Blue Reserves)
Entire Regiment, Companies A–K
   I (Abbot Guards)
   K (Industrial Guards)

9th Regiment
Entire Regiment, Companies A–K
   C (City Grays)

20th Regiment
Companies A–F, K
   A (Corn Exchange Guard)
   B (Grey Reserves)
   C (W. L. McDowell Guards)
   D (Corn Exchange Guard)
   E (Revenue Guards)
   F (Corn Exchange Guard)
   K (2nd Company Revenue
      Guards)

21st Regiment
Company B
    A (A. C. Washington Greys)
    C (Philadelphia City Guards)
    F (3rd Company Washington
       Greys)

25th Regiment
Entire Regiment, Companies A–K

National Guard Regiment
Companies A–H, K

Baldwin Light Infantry
Companies A, B, G, H

Two Independent Infantry Companies (J. L. Wilson and R. Van
Valkenburg)

Three Artillery Batteries (Landis,
Miller, Robertson)

1863 Militia

20th Regiment
Companies A–F, H–M

31st Regiment
Companies A, B, C, E, K

32nd Regiment (Grey Reserves)
Entire Regiment, Companies A–K
    L (Frishmuth's Battery)

33rd Regiment (Blue Reserves)
Entire Regiment, Companies A–K

40th Regiment (1st Coal Trade)
Entire Regiment, Companies A–K
    G (2nd Company Hamilton
       Rifles)

44th Regiment (Merchants' Regiment)
Entire Regiment, Companies A–K

45th Regiment (1st Union
League)
Entire Regiment, Companies A–K

49th Regiment (2nd Corn
Exchange)
Companies A–D, F–I

51st Regiment (2nd Coal Trade)
Entire Regiment, Companies A–L

52nd Regiment (2nd Union
League)
Entire Regiment, Companies A–K

59th Regiment (3rd Union
League)
Entire Regiment, Companies A–K

60th Regiment (Victualers' Regiment)
Entire Regiment, Companies A–C,
E–G, I
    1st Battalion (Ramsey's)
    Companies C and E

3rd Battalion (1st Pennsylvania
Chasseurs)
Entire Battalion, Companies A–E

Five Independent Infantry Companies (Spear, Mann, Taylor, German, Campbell)

1st Cavalry Battalion
Company A

Three Independent Cavalry Companies
    Hammell's (Dana Troop)

Randall's (1st City Troop)
Rich's

**Five Independent Artillery
Batteries**
Miller's
Landis's
Woodward's
Montgomery's (Common-
wealth Artillery)
Fitzki's (2nd Keystone Artillery)

1864 Militia

Southard's Independent Infantry
Company

Stroud's Independent Cavalry
Company (Railroad Troop)

Keystone Battery

Listed here are published regimental histories for units primarily from Philadelphia. Many are available in libraries; many have been reprinted within the past two decades by publishers of Civil War books.

Bates, Samuel P. *History of Pennsylvania Volunteers, 1861–5.* 5 vols. Harrisburg: B. Singerly, State Printer, 1869–1871. Reprint (10 vols., with Index, 4 vols.), Wilmington, NC: Broadfoot, 1993–1994. (For general histories and rosters of all Pennsylvania units.)

Brewer, Abraham T. *History Sixty-first Regiment Pennsylvania Volunteers, 1861–1865.* Pittsburgh: Art Engraving and Printing, 1911.

Chamberlin, Thomas. *History of the One Hundred and Fiftieth Regiment Pennsylvania Volunteers, Second Regiment, Bucktail Brigade.* Philadelphia: J. B. Lippincott, 1895. Second ed., Philadelphia: F. McManus Jr., 1905.

Gottfried, Bradley M. *Stopping Pickett: The History of the Philadelphia Brigade.* Shippensburg, PA: White Mane, 1999.

Gracey, Samuel L. *Annals of the Sixth Pennsylvania Cavalry.* Philadelphia: E. H. Butler, 1868.

Hagerty, Edward. *Collis' Zouaves: The 114th Pennsylvania Volunteers in the Civil War.* Baton Rouge: Louisiana State University Press, 1997.

History of the Third Pennsylvania Cavalry, Sixtieth Regiment Pennsylvania Volunteers in the American Civil War, 1861–1865. Philadelphia: Franklin, 1905.

Kirk, Charles H. *History of the Fifteenth Pennsylvania Volunteer Cavalry, Which Was Recruited and Known as the Anderson Cavalry in the Rebellion of 1861–1865.* Philadelphia, 1906.

Maier, Larry B. *Rough and Regular: A History of Philadelphia's 119th Regiment of Pennsylvania Volunteer Infantry, The Gray Reserves.* Shippensburg, PA: Burd Street, 1997.

McDermott, Anthony W. *Brief History of the Sixty-ninth Regiment of Pennsylvania Veteran Volunteers, from Its Formation Until Final Muster Out of the United States Service.* Philadelphia: D. J. Gallagher, 1889.

Mulholland, St. Clair A. *The Story of the 116th Regiment Pennsylvania Volunteers in the War of the Rebellion, The Record of a Gallant Campaign.* Philadelphia: F. McManus Jr., 1903.

Myers, John C. *A Daily Journal of the 192d Reg't. Penn'a. Volunteers, Commanded by Colonel William B. Thomas, in the Service of the United States for One Hundred Days.* Philadelphia: Crissy & Markley, 1864.

Nachtigill, Hermann. *Geschichte des 75sten Regiments, Pa. Vols.* Philadelphia: C. B. Kretchman, 1886.

Smith, John L. *History of the Corn Exchange Regiment 118th Pennsylvania Volunteers, from Their First Engagement at Antietam to Appomattox, to Which Is Added a Record of Its Organization and a Complete Roster.* Philadelphia: Author, 1888, 1892, 1905.

Strong, William W. *History of the 121st Regiment Pennsylvania Volunteers, by the Survivors' Association. "An Account from the Ranks."* Philadelphia: Burk & McFetridge, 1893. Rev. ed., Philadelphia: Catholic Standard and Times, 1906.

Vautier, John W. *History of the 88th Pennsylvania Volunteers in the War for the Union, 1861–1865.* Philadelphia: J. B. Lippincott, 1894.

Ward, George W. *History of the Second Pennsylvania Veteran Heavy Artillery (112th Regiment Pennsylvania Volunteers), from 1861 to 1866, Including the Provisional Second Penn'a. Heavy Artillery.* Philadelphia: George W. Ward, 1904.

Ward, Joseph R. C. *History of the One Hundred and Sixth Regiment Pennsylvania Volunteers, 2d Brigade, 2d Division, 2d Corps, 1861–1865.* Philadelphia: Grant, Faires & Rodgers, 1883. Rev. ed., Philadelphia: F. McManus Jr., 1906.

Woodward, Evan M. *History of the One Hundred and Ninety-eighth Pennsylvania Volunteers, Being a Complete Record of the Regiment, with Its Camps, Marches and Battles, Together with the Personal Record of Every Officer and Man During His Term of Service.* Trenton, NJ: MacCrellish & Quigley, 1884.

———. *History of the Third Pennsylvania Reserve.* Trenton, NJ: MacCrellish & Quigley, 1883.

————. *Our Campaigns; Or, The Marches, Bivouacs, Battles, Incidents of Camp Life and History of Our Regiment During Its Three Years Term of Service*. Philadelphia: John E. Potter, 1865. (2nd Reserves.)

Wray, William J. *History of the Twenty-third Pennsylvania Volunteer Infantry, Birney's Zouaves, Three Months and Three Years Service, Civil War, 1861–1865*. Philadelphia, 1904.

United States Colored Troops Recruited in Philadelphia

The eleven black regiments formed at Camp William Penn were credited to Pennsylvania, but most included sizable contingents of men from other states as well. For these units, no single company was recruited exclusively within the city. The companies listed here all contained men from within the city limits in addition to soldiers from other counties and states.

3rd United States Colored Troops
Entire regiment, Companies A–K, primarily recruited in city

6th United States Colored Troops
Companies A–K

8th United States Colored Troops
Companies A, B, C, E, F, G, I, K

22nd United States Colored Troops
Companies A–K

24th United States Colored Troops
Companies A, B, D, E, F, G, H, I, K

25th United States Colored Troops
Companies B, C, D, E, F

32nd United States Colored Troops
Companies A, C, D, E, F

41st United States Colored Troops
Companies A, C, D, E, H, I, K

43rd United States Colored Troops
Companies A, C, E, F

45th United States Colored Troops
Companies D, E, F, G, H, I, K

127th United States Colored Troops
Companies A, I, K

Bibliography

Alotta, Robert I. *Mermaids, Monasteries, Cherokees and Custer: The Stories Behind Philadelphia Street Names*. Chicago: Bonus Books, 1990.

Bazelon, Bruce S. *Horstmann's: The Enterprise of Military Equipage*. Manassas, VA: REF Typesetting & Publishing, 1997.

Bazelon, Bruce S., and William F. McGuinn. *A Directory of American Military Goods Dealers & Makers 1785–1915*. Comb. ed. Manassas, VA: REF Typesetting & Publishing, 1999.

Beyer, George R. *Guide to the State Historical Markers of Pennsylvania*. Harrisburg: Pennsylvania Historical and Museum Commission, 1991.

Binder, Frederick M. "Pennsylvania Negro Regiments in the Civil War." *Journal of Negro History* 37 (1952): 383–417.

———. "Philadelphia's Free Military School." *Pennsylvania History* 17 (1950): 101–13.

Blockson, Charles L. *Hippocrene Guide to the Underground Railroad*. New York: Hippocrene Books, 1994.

———. *Philadelphia's Guide: African-American State Historical Markers*. Philadelphia: Charles L. Blockson African-American Collection and William Penn Foundation, 1992.

Bonsall, Joseph H., and Samuel L. Smedley. *Map of the City of Philadelphia According to Confirmed Plans & Official Surveys Photographically Reproduced from the Large Drawings for an Index to the Complete Atlas of the City*. Philadelphia, 1862.

Burek, Deborah M., ed. *Cemeteries of the U.S.: A Guide to Contact Information for U.S. Cemeteries and Their Records*. Detroit: Gale Research, 1994.

Cantor, George. *Historic Black Landmarks: A Traveler's Guide*. Detroit: Visible Ink, 1991.

Cotter, John L., Daniel G. Roberts, and Michael Parrington. *The Buried Past: An Archaeological History of Philadelphia*. Philadelphia: University of Pennsylvania Press, 1992.

Cox, J. Lee, Jr. *Submerged Cultural Resources Investigations, Delaware River Main Channel Deepening Project, Delaware, New Jersey, and Pennsylvania*. Prepared for the Greeley-Polhemus Group by Dolan Research, 1994.

Dorwart, Jeffery M. *Fort Mifflin of Philadelphia: An Illustrated History*. Philadelphia: University of Pennsylvania Press, 1998.

DuBarry, William. "Five Forgotten Shipbuilders of the American Clyde." Paper presented to the Philadelphia Section of the Society of Naval Architects and Marine Engineers, Philadelphia, PA, 1997.

Edwards, William B. *Civil War Guns*. Secaucus, NJ: Castle Books, 1982.

The First 300: The Amazing and Rich History of Lower Merion. Ardmore, PA: Lower Merion Historical Society, 2000.

Freedley, Edwin T. *Philadelphia and Its Manufactures: A Hand-Book Exhibiting the Development, Variety, and Statistics of the Manufacturing Industry of Philadelphia in 1857*. Philadelphia: Edward Young, 1858.

Gallery, John A., ed. *Philadelphia Architecture: A Guide to the City*. Cambridge, MA: MIT Press, 1984.

Gallman, J. Matthew. *Mastering Wartime: A Social History of Philadelphia During the Civil War*. Cambridge, MA: Cambridge University Press, 1990.

Gluckman, Arcadi. *Identifying Old U.S. Muskets, Rifles and Carbines*. New York: Bonanza Books, 1965.

Homan, Wayne E. "Griffen Designs a Cannon." *Philadelphia Inquirer Magazine*, October 17, 1965.

Jackson, Joseph. *Encyclopedia of Philadelphia*. 4 vols. Harrisburg: National Historical Association, 1933.

Klein, Esther M. *Fairmount Park: A History and a Guidebook*. Bryn Mawr: Harcum Junior College Press, 1974.

MacKay, Winnifred. "Philadelphia During the Civil War, 1861–1865." *Pennsylvania Magazine of History and Biography* (1946): 3–51.

Magner, Blake A. *At Peace with Honor: The Civil War Burials of Laurel Hill Cemetery, Philadelphia, Pennsylvania*. Collingswood, NJ: CW Historicals, 1997.

Moore, James. *History of the Cooper Shop Volunteer Refreshment Saloon*. Philadelphia: James B. Rodgers, 1866.

Sauers, Richard A. *Advance the Colors! Pennsylvania Civil War Battle Flags*. 2 vols. Lebanon, PA: Sowers Printing Company for the Capitol Preservation Committee, 1987–1991.

Scharf, J. Thomas, and Thompson Westcott. *History of Philadelphia, 1609–1884*. 3 vols. Philadelphia: L. H. Everts, 1884.

Silverstone, Paul H. *Warships of the Civil War Navies*. Annapolis, MD: Naval Institute Press, 1989.

Smedley, Samuel L. *Map of Philadelphia Photographically Reproduced from the 25 Large Sectional Drawings Contained in Smedley's Atlas of Philadelphia*. Philadelphia: J. L. Smith, 1861.

Smith, Philip C. F. *Philadelphia on the River*. Philadelphia: University of Pennsylvania Press, 1986.

Taylor, Frank H. *Philadelphia in the Civil War 1861–1865*. Philadelphia: Dunlap, 1913.

Vogel, Morris J. *Cultural Connections: Museums and Libraries of Philadelphia and the Delaware Valley*. Philadelphia: Temple University Press, 1991.

Webster, Richard J. *Philadelphia Preserved: Catalog of the Historic American Buildings Survey*. Philadelphia: Temple University Press, 1976. Second ed., 1981.

Weigley, Russell F., ed. *Philadelphia: A 300-Year History*. New York: W. W. Norton, 1982.

Wert, Jeffrey D. "Camp William Penn and the Black Soldier." *Pennsylvania History* 46 (1979): 335–46.

Whiteman, Maxwell. *Gentlemen in Crisis: The First Century of the Union League of Philadelphia, 1862–1962*. Philadelphia: Winchell, 1975.

The WPA Guide to Philadelphia, Compiled by the Federal Writers' Project of the Works Progress Administration for the Commonwealth of Pennsylvania. 1937. Reprint, Philadelphia: University of Pennsylvania Press, 1988, 1991.

Index